THE TEMPTATION TO BE GOOD

By A. Powell Davies

AMERICAN DESTINY
THE FAITH OF AN UNREPENTANT LIBERAL
AMERICA'S REAL RELIGION
MAN'S VAST FUTURE
THE TEMPTATION TO BE GOOD

THE TEMPTATION
TO BE GOOD

A BOOK OF
UNCONVENTIONAL SERMONS

BY A. POWELL DAVIES

FARRAR, STRAUS AND YOUNG

NEW YORK

To those who have come to me
  in their distress,
Doubting but still believing,
  Wounded but not defeated,
Showing me how limitless is
  human possibility:

These above all others
  have been my teachers,
And to them I dedicate
  this book.

FOREWORD

This book is intended for those who are doubtful that religion can do anything to help them but who very much wish that it could. Those who already know what they believe, and are contented with it, will not mind, I hope, if I speak to less confident people in an untraditional way.

My pulpit in Washington, D. C., is unusually free. My congregation, although occasionally apprehensive, expects me to say exactly what I think, and I have formed the habit of doing so. This has enabled me to deal with the problems of modern life without having to defend conventional opinions.

The twenty-one sermons which compose the book are concerned with a rather wide variety of subjects, but all are centered in the quest of the individual for spiritual reality and authentic moral guidance. Too many people are trying to contend with the very real problems of a vividly real world with nothing real in their own inner lives. Such efforts are misdirected. It is possible, without believing anything that strains credulity, to have a real religion. To that possibility, this book is a modest contribution.

My thanks are due to Miss Jane Grey Wheeler, my assistant, for transcribing these sermons from my notes and for patient cooperation in the editing. Two of the sermons, in a shorter form, appeared in the magazine, *Freedom & Union;* four others, in whole or in part, were printed for subscribers to the regular monthly series of published sermons which go out from my Church. To my congregation, surely the most responsive and encouraging to be found anywhere, I express once more my deep indebtedness.

A. POWELL DAVIES.

CONTENTS

I

To Some Who Feel Lost

IT IS RELATED *of a certain traveler, somewhere in northern Vermont, that after driving in uncertainty for a while, he became convinced that he was on the wrong road, and so, at the first village, came to a halt.*

Calling one of the villagers to the car window, he said, "Friend, I need help. I'm lost." The villager looked at him for a moment. "Do you know where you are?" he asked. "Yes," said the traveler, "I saw the name of the village as I entered." The man nodded his head. "Do you know where you want to go?" "Yes," the traveler replied, and named his destination. The villager looked away for a moment, ruminating. "You ain't lost," he said at last, "you just need directions."

1

The Temptation to Be Good

SOME FEW YEARS ago, I received a call in my office from
a man who was in Washington on a mission of some sort
from a European country. Exactly what his business was
I do not now remember, nor why he took the time to
come to see me. What I do recall about our interview is
that we went over the sad state of the world for a few
minutes, and then my visitor leaned back in his chair and
said, as much to himself as to me, "You know, at every
level, people are almost good; they are tempted to be
good, but they resist the temptation."

Then, quite casually, he went on to something else.
What it was, I have forgotten. It was a hurried interview,
sandwiched in between appointments, and I might not
have remembered it at all if it had not been for that one
remark. "At every level, people are almost good; they are
tempted to be good, but they resist the temptation."
These were words I would never forget.

How true it is! From the level of rulers of nations down
to the daily life of the lowliest peasant, people are "almost good." They feel drawn towards it. They are aware
of goodness as a possible choice. They feel it as a temptation—a temptation to leave the dreary paths of disappointment and frustration and live as they really want to
live—but they resist it. And so the world falls apart, not
through evil, deliberately chosen evil, but because its
people resist the temptation to be good.

[3]

It may seem at first an odd way of putting it—temptation to be *good*. We are more accustomed to think of
temptation in connection with evil. It is virtue, we say,
that is tempted: tempted to yield to the attractions of
vice. We imagine virtue as the normal state of things
from which we are tempted to depart. Life is good, the
world is good, people are good, everything is good—until
temptation brings its interferences. Then, because we give
in, good is replaced by evil.

But is it as simple as that? For a long while now, there
have been many who supposed so, but they may be
wrong. Modern-minded people are usually not convinced
by the Garden of Eden narrative, in which Adam and
Eve, as first parents, were expelled from an earthly para-
dise because they were tempted away from virtue. But
they are under the spell of such illusions as Wordsworth's,
who tells us that "heaven lies about us in our infancy,"
and that "trailing clouds of glory do we come, from God
who is our home." And thus they postulate virtue as the
happy condition from which, in our growth towards
adulthood, we gradually fall away, whereas in actual fact
it is a condition to which we never quite attain.

No one who has really observed the human infant ac-
curately would maintain that "heaven lies about us in our
infancy." Wordsworth didn't know what he was talking
about. Even the most casual of baby-sitters could have
enlightened him. Quite evidently, Wordsworth was a
much better observer of nature in other places than he
was in a nursery. For whatever may lie about us in our
infancy, heaven is not the word for it. The young human
animal can indeed be quite attractive on occasions, and I
have felt the power of that attraction; but that he trails
clouds of glory I resolutely deny.

I also deny his virtue. The human infant is neither virtuous nor vicious; for the most part, he is just a hungry little animal to whom, for the time being, neither virtue nor vice has the slightest meaning. After a while, he will cease to be an infant and will practice both, and neither will have, nor ever did have, priority over the other. For the fact is that virtue is *not* our original state, and neither is vice. Good and evil are both potential. We can be drawn to the one or to the other, to either or to both. We can vacillate between them. We can be tempted not only to evil but to good. Let us admit, then, that virtue is an attainment, not an original possession, and to reach it we have to go forward to something we never had, not back to something we have lost.

It is quite correct, therefore, to speak of being tempted to be good. We are drawn towards goodness just as we are drawn towards evil. When we do badly, we have not only followed an impulse towards badness, we have resisted the attraction of goodness. And this is what people are doing all the while, just as my visitor remarked, "at every level" from that of the great of the earth down to the lowliest and humblest.

We should talk less about good people and bad people, as though they were distinct categories into which everyone can somehow be fitted. We should recognize that most people, and perhaps nearly all people, are "almost good." They do wrong only by suppressing a desire to do right. They do right only by resisting an attraction towards wrong. The temptation, if the word is used in this more accurate way, may be seen to come from two directions, not from one, and a choice must be made between them.

Nor is it true that the pull in one direction is always

strong, and in the other, weak. The temptation to be good is frequently a powerful one. So powerful, indeed, that if we choose evil we have to pretend the opposite; we must excuse ourselves, "rationalize", as the psychologists have taught us to call it, and make wrong seem right, or at least partly right. If this is too difficult, we take refuge in the belief—an insincere one—that neither good nor evil is important, that life is without moral significance, that the battle is a sham one, that there are no values whatever in the end except expediency.

That is what some of our philosophers have done. Yet, in doing it they have had to put up a constant, noisy fight to keep themselves convinced. Schopenhauer, for instance, telling us that nothing really matters but insisting upon it so loudly and defiantly that we have to ask ourselves what it is that he is trying to shout down, to browbeat, to cudgel into submission. Something is talking back at him; indeed, the whole of life is talking back at him. The struggle that he calls fictitious holds him in so firm a grip that he cries out from the pain of it. Good and evil will not let him go. He says they do not finally exist, yet he is forever preoccupied with them. Their reality is the one fact with which, willy-nilly, he must contend.

Or we might take one of Schopenhauer's disciples—for such he was if we trace back the factors that molded him —Adolf Hitler. He, too, was cynical concerning good and evil. Yet, he was tortured by them. The evil that he chose he had to justify as good. His need for self-justification was acute; we might even call it morbid. It was the measure, of course, of his temptation to be good. No matter how much he might deride goodness in its more conventional forms, or laugh at such virtues as keeping a promise or being generous to an adversary, he had to find a category in which he, himself, could seem to be good. That he was an evil man and an enemy of goodness, he indignantly denied. On the contrary, he looked upon his personal virtue as heroic.

And so we might continue. I do not suppose there is a gangster in America, or a corrupt political boss, or a would-be dictator, or anyone else regarded as inimical to goodness, who does not justify himself as somehow virtuous. He will admit, no doubt, that, judged by ordinary standards, he may be less than perfect, but he will always point to something that he thinks should justify him, and to other things he counts as meritorious.

That is one side of the matter. So powerful is the temptation to be good that those who resist it nevertheless pay tribute to it, if only in hypocrisy and self-deception. Yet, there are times, of course, when they see the truth. What they justify in moments of defiance rebukes them in the lonely hours of self-recognition and remorse. For people do not seem to themselves always the same thing, and self-love is always ready to turn itself into self-hate.

It can also vacillate and become something which is neither the one nor the other, but which saps away the joy of life and poisons all contentment. Most of the time, that is how people try to get along. They are assisted in it by prevailing attitudes; the attitude, for instance, that goodness, in spite of its attractiveness, is rather disappointing if you give in to it. To be good is to be out of step with the world. As Mark Twain put it, "Be good and you will be lonesome."

Or again, a generation ago, goodness was thought to be more appropriate to women than to men; it was not quite masculine. Now, of course, it is not quite feminine, either.

Women have gained an equal right to be bad. I hope no feminist among my readers will be offended at my saying this, for I believe completely in the equality of the sexes. Indeed, not only do I believe in the equal *right* of women . to be bad; I believe in their equal capacity!

The truth about goodness is that it is just as masculine, and just as feminine, or—to put the matter quite impartially and very simply—just as human as anything opposed to it. Evil is seldom strength; it is almost always weakness. When we have taken the trouble to understand goodness a little better and have found the courage to resist prevailing attitudes, we can see that far from goodness being suited only to the timid or the weak, it is possible only to the courageous and the strong. That is why we are afraid of it. We invert our values in the effort to excuse ourselves, but in our hearts we know that we are not excused.

What is it that makes people turn away from the temptation to be good? Let us suppose that it is the right and wrong of some public question, some cause of justice that cries out to be served. We are tempted to see the truth, and therefore to speak it, to recognize injustice, and therefore to condemn it. There is power in this temptation. It invites us to feel clean and decent, to look upon excuses as beneath us, to be forthright, honest, candid with ourselves—yes, and to strike a blow for what we know is right.

But if we do that, ah! how shall we stand in the opinion of others? It will make things hard for us. People we like will be against us. People whose esteem we want will disesteem us. And thinking thus, we let the moment pass, and presently our backs are turned—turned on the temptation to be good.

We did not stop to think that all those other people

were doing exactly as we were. They, too, had been tempted to take the right side; they gave up for the same reasons that we did. If the cause goes unserved, if injustice remains, if wrong prevails instead of right, it is not because people were divided as groups, some of them good people, others bad. No, it is because most of the people, those who really decided the matter, were *almost* good. As my visitor had put it, they were "tempted to be good," but had "resisted the temptation."

That is what happens everywhere, in palaces and parliaments, in senates and assemblies, in cabinet meetings and councils—everywhere that great decisions are registered. The struggle is seldom between good and evil, but between good and almost good. Truth trembles on the tongue, is almost spoken, and then not quite spoken. Everyone present seems relieved. It saved embarrassment. Yet, everyone is also disappointed, deeply and secretly disappointed. It has happened again! The same old surrender, the same old defeat! It need not have happened. Sometimes, thank God, it does not happen. Truth really is spoken, and in spite of embarrassment, even in spite of protest and dismay, all who hear it know that humanity has been lifted a little higher in that moment, and thus, there is more of hope for all of us. Some one has been tempted, successfully tempted, not to evil but to good.

That is what happened to the world's great prophets, the exemplars and the moral pioneers. A Socrates is tempted to speak the truth and he speaks it. An Amos is tempted to declare that true religion is concerned with righteousness, not ritual sacrifice, and he does declare it. A Jesus is tempted to denounce hypocrisy, and does denounce it. And thus, for all mankind there comes to be a higher range of possibility. What these men did, others may do. Human stature has been raised by those who yielded to the nobler impulse, the temptation to be good.

But, as my friend said, too many of us are "almost good." We resist the temptation. I was told not long since by a United States Senator of how near the Senate came, one day, to rejecting a bill that the majority of members knew to be bad. In the end, however, it was not rejected; the Senate passed it. He went, this Senator, from one of his colleagues to another, asking each in turn why he had voted as he did. None of them said they voted from conviction. They had wanted to reject the bill; they almost did reject it: but in the situation which they saw existing, they became afraid. Instead of doing the right thing, they did the expedient thing—or what they thought was such. How often does this happen in the affairs of nations? How often is a great decision almost right? How often are men tempted, men who have been given the people's trust, to follow their convictions, to be honest, to do right, and then resist the temptation—the temptation to be good?

But this happens, too, in humbler places, in homes and among friends and in all the habitats of common life. Here are two people, we will suppose, a man and his wife whose lives are growing apart. There are thousands of such couples, unfortunately, and, as every minister knows, so often it is unnecessary, pitiful, and no less foolish than sad. But here they are, these two, each embattled against the other. Each is sure, and insists upon it, that although, of course, it takes two to make a quarrel and there is always some wrong on both sides, yet in this case, this unusual case, this really unique case, all the substantial wrong is really on *one* side, that is to say, the *other* side. And so it goes, on and on and on.

Yet, there are moments when one of them feels—and sometimes both of them—the temptation to be generous, the sudden outreach of sympathy, the humbling recognition of what he is doing—of what she is doing—and of the folly of being harsh in a world that is too harsh already, throwing away happiness as though happiness were easy to find.

The temptation—it is there! You can see it in their eyes, in a change of voice, in a moment's quietness when they look down at the ground and avoid each other's gaze. Then comes the resistance, the eyes glaze over, the voice hardens. Self-justification begins to speak again—and pride! Yes, pride, surely the last enemy humanity will overcome. And so the temptation is resisted—the temptation to be good.

What cruelty is there anywhere that might not have been kindness—that almost *was* kindness? What brutality that was not tempted to be gentle? What obstinacy that did not melt a little and begin to relent? Where was there a temptation ever—to evil—that came alone, that was not accompanied by a temptation to be good?

So near do we come to what we yearn for, and yet we turn away. We hunger and thirst after righteousness, and when it comes within our reach, we reject it, and so we are hungry and thirsty still. What we love, we resist, and what we hate, we take to our hearts. Then we wonder why the world is full of heartaches. When shall we learn? —we who are not evil, we who are almost good? We come so close, at times, so very close that heaven itself must marvel that we miss our goal.

But we are afraid: afraid lest life should touch us with its terrifying greatness. And we fear for the opinion of others, clothing us in acceptance and respectability, and for our place in the world, warm and sheltered, bricked about with petty cowardice and roofed with layer upon layer of cherished littleness. Against all this, what can goodness say that truly tempts us? Goodness, with its gentle pleading and its softly whispered words?

Ah, but it does tempt us! It tempts us to live the lives we were born to live, to leave the caves of refuge in which our souls are suffocating and go out—out where the sky of truth is wide above us, out where the air we breathe is clean and we can breathe it deep, out where we belong in the world of the honest and the real. Yes, and we are tempted, too, to kindness, to charity, to generosity; to patience, to forbearance, to sympathy; to simplicity, sincerity, humility.

"At every level people are almost good." That is what Jesus knew. They said he was the friend of bad people, of "publicans and sinners." But they were wrong. The publicans and sinners were not bad people; they were the "almost good." So were the Scribes and Pharisees, and the rulers at Jerusalem; and so was Simon Peter, so brave in promises, so craven in denials. So even was Judas, who, having betrayed his Master, found nothing left to live for and took his own life. So were they all, and the gospel of Jesus was preached to the "almost good."

It is true that they rejected him. Nevertheless, they were not able to forget him. Goodness cannot be forgotten, and in that is our hope. We are tempted not only to evil but to good. Goodness powerfully attracts us. Virtue, even when we turn our backs upon it, shines so brightly from behind that we see the shape of our lives cast down in our shadows. The truth cannot be hidden from us. We know. The excuses are fluent upon our lips. Yes, but we know. We speak defiance, we shout denials, we surrender at last to despair. Ah, but we still know.

And what is it that we know? We know that we fear goodness, but that we fear because we love. The good, the true, the just, the gentle—these have claimed us. We belong to them. No matter what the evil deeds we do, we never love them. It is goodness that we love. We love it with a love that will not let us go.

2

Of Life and Coffee Spoons

ACCORDING TO Mr. Clifton Fadiman, the life of the average man "tends to assume the form of a longish doze," interrupted by fits and starts of "bewildered semi-alertness." Not that we invite this semi-alertness, even when it happens to us; on the contrary, we try to head it off. We will invent a hundred ways of obstructing self-awareness, says Mr. Fadiman, especially if it is likely to lead to our becoming completely awake to life and therefore under the necessity of facing some difficult but insistent questions, such as What am I? What am I doing here? Where am I going? What does it all mean? Am I really living the way I want to live or just going on by habit?

Is life more like making the morning train in which every commuter is meaningless, inquires Mr. Fadiman, or is it more like wandering in a wood where every tree is a mystery? "Am I complete because I have a pocket-book, a social security number, a last will and testament? Or have I lost something I cannot put a name to? Do I know my way around—or don't I?"

All of which he writes by way of introduction to a very delightful book of lunatic cartoons by Abner Dean, the title of which is "What Am I Doing Here?" The lunacy, of course, is not Mr. Dean's; he merely depicts the life he sees around him. In our more observant moments—if we have any—we are likely, I think, to share Mr. Dean's view of the world we are living in, and also Mr. Fadiman's opinion that "the life of the average man tends to assume the form of a longish doze." Not many people are really living; most of them are just sleeping life off.

If our lives were thoroughly conscious—we need not say sane, but just conscious—how could it happen that so many people devote themselves to the meaningless, and do almost nothing to arrest the idiotic course of events which is certain, unless more people come awake, to issue in disaster?

The majority are thinking the same worn out thoughts, attending to the same irrelevant aims, enjoying the same unearned repose as in a former time when the fate of the world seemed safer. Leaders and people, both—or, at least, far too many of them and for far too much of the time—are acting as though no new exertions were necessary. Political corruption is not so much a conscious betrayal as the continuance of a drowsy habit. Greed is not intentional; it is just a sleep-walking sort of avarice. People are not doing wrong by design, deliberately imperilling the moral basis of our national security; they are evil in a dreamy way, unrighteous in their sleep.

What is it that happens to people, so that instead of living their lives consciously and deliberately in accordance with their chosen aims, they allow themselves to drift along in semi-consciousness, neither quite awake nor quite asleep? Thomas Wolfe asks this question, in a story told in one of his posthumous books. He asks it in a sort of parable, through the musings of Old James, a man of affairs who at the opening of the story, looks "upon the faded gilt of morning with a baffled eye." Where had his life gone to, he asks, the passion and fire of his youth, the faith, the hope, the clean belief of fifty years ago? All

gone! Even the "patient, hard confusion of honest doubt"
had somehow been dissolved away and in its place was
the "vile smirk of a passive acceptance . . . the fattied
heart no longer sound enough for battle, the clouded and
beclamoured mind no longer clear enough for truth, the
bleared eye murked with rotten mockeries." *

Old James cannot remember what had happened, or
when and where. All that he can be sure of is that the
wonder and belief of his earlier years had somehow been
dissipated, and instead, he found wearying vulgarities and
an empty show. Somewhere along the line he had sold
out and had scarcely noticed it. From that time on, he
had settled down into a long doze—a profitable doze,
counted in dollars and cents; and active, too, like sleep-
walking—but he himself was not awake. He had missed
life, and life had passed him by.

From Thomas Wolfe, let us turn to T. S. Eliot, who, in
the opinion of many (though not in mine), is the representative poet of the modern age. In any case, the poem
by which he is best known is representative of the malady
we have been describing. "Let us go then, you and I,"
begins the Love Song of J. Alfred Prufrock, "When the
evening is spread out against the sky—" Then comes the
third line, shocking, discordant, full of the cacophony of
modern life: "Like a patient etherized upon a table."

Thus the poem proceeds, depicting modern man as a
sort of Hamlet without the dignity of Hamlet, an absent-
minded, obtuse and almost ridiculous sort of Hamlet, too
meaningless to be tragic. He is lost, is modern man, full of
dreams, but with no power to live a dream. Everything
about him ends up with a feeling of inconsequence. After

---

* "The Lion at Morning," in *The Hills Beyond*, Thomas Wolfe,
Harper, N. Y., 1941.

all, it didn't really matter. Not necessary to ask what "it" refers to; nothing matters.

It is in this poem that the well-known lines occur,

> For I have known them all, already, known them all,
> Have known the evenings, mornings, afternoons,
> I have measured out my life with coffee-spoons.

There we have it! The smallest, most prudential common measure available—a coffee-spoon! Life measured out in coffee-spoons, emotion administered with a medicine-dropper! No greatness of desire, no audacities in aim and purpose, no greatness even in the questions asked. Just one coffee-spoonful of awareness; not enough for waking up, just enough to stay above the borderline of sleep.

And there is our trouble, from the affairs of nations down to those of homes and individuals. No great beliefs, no surrender of pettiness for great ends, no boldness of design, no "all thy heart, and all thy soul, and all thy strength" in anything.

Let us admit that even Hitlerism, evil as it was, represented for many a revolt against this half-aliveness. If righteousness commanded no allegiance, if goodness had lost its zest, if beneficence was trivial and picayune, iniquity would at least be colossal and adventurous. It would become the new religion, the new righteousness. He, Hitler, would make it so.

After his downfall, the communists took up his role. Their plans are even larger, their conspiracy ubiquitous. But the communists are at least awake; that much we shall have to grant them. While we have dozed along, they have been unceasing in activity. And to many, the attraction of communism has been its energy, its aliveness and alertness.

Meanwhile, our own great principles, which should define our purposes, we have slept with, sluggishly, muttering of freedom in a "longish doze." We have doled out freedom in a coffee-spoon diplomacy. That is what we did between the wars. A coffee-spoonful of neutrality about Ethiopia, a coffee-spoonful of non-intervention when Europe began to go to pieces. One coffee-spoonful after another, until at last we had to throw our coffee-spoons away and salvage our freedoms with oceans of treasure and rivers of blood.

Where was the greatness of aim, the passion for liberty, the indignation at injustice? Where even was the abhorrence of brutality, the resentment at depravity? Where were any of the things by which the souls of men and nations live? They were measured down—that is where they were—to measuring cups that we could dip in with our coffee-spoons.

But let us turn from nations to the lives of individuals. Nations are made up of individuals, and the behavior of a society reflects the standards of its individual members. One picks up a novel, written in accordance with contemporary formula. Every man in the book distrusts every other man, and all the men distrust their women. Each character, in turn, looks at every other character through narrowed eyelids. There is no expectation of honesty or loyalty. There is no love—only dominance. That is the most to be expected—dominance. The emotional question is who shall dominate whom? No one dares to love anybody; it is too much of a risk. Take what you can get. Have a little barnyard fun. Don't look for love; don't think of beauty—or even rapture. Just the thrill, then the frustration. Finally, the boredom. And now, try it again, somewhere else—till boredom comes once more.

In this description, I have in mind an actual novel, a best-seller of a recent year, but it would apply to many novels. If these stories, or even some of them, actually do reflect the emotional life of today, one need not wonder at so many marriages falling apart, or trouble to inquire why love between spouses has no faith and fealty in it. It is a love measured out in coffee-spoons. Nor is there any true aliveness in it. A human being is all he is—what he is as a person, not just as glands and nervous system—and emotional experience of this sort leaves most of him excluded, condemned to Mr. Fadiman's "longish doze."

How can you make a marriage out of the maxim that one coffee-spoonful must match another, and that the thing to watch is that nobody gets a coffee-spoonful ahead? Where are the spontaneities, the whole-heartedness, the simple gladness of an outgoing love?

And the same is true of other human relationships. How much alive can you be with your personal self cut off and insulated? How much actual living are you doing if you quench your sympathies and measure out your generosities? These were questions, apparently, which much troubled the mind of Jesus. Being so ardently alive himself, he was impatient at the petty pieties, the trivial, measured-out righteousness of many who came to hear him. He talked about "life abundant" and said he came to bring that kind of life. In other words, he wanted to make people more alive. But most of them were afraid, then as now, to be more alive. It was safer to be only partly alive. It took less effort, less courage. After all, if you were fully alive, you were more sharply aware of pain as well as of happiness. You noticed the things that were wrong, you were disturbed at injuries to other people. It might be better to be a little sleepy, to invite a moral torpor, and thus be noticed less and not so prone to deal in matters controversial.

Yet, Jesus insisted that people were hungry and thirsty for life. As indeed they were—both were and are. But they seem to know it only in "fits and starts of bewildered semi-alertness." They want to see great meanings in life without inviting greatness into their own lives. As though one could find great purpose in the world without following worthy aims in his own way of living! Should liars complain because they cannot find eternal verities? Can beauty be loved by those who feel no pain at ugliness? What marvel is it that half-alive minds find only denial and negation? Why should it be otherwise? Can half-closed hearts know love? What room can they make for what they are too small to contain?

How, then, does a person come alive? The answer is a rigorous one: there is no miracle. God has given us already what most of us pray for; what we need is to call it forth. We can begin almost anywhere: with some new cause, perhaps, waiting to be served, some harsh injustice crying out to be remedied. Or we may begin just with being kinder, allowing imagination to quicken sympathy. We can begin in many ways, or in almost any way, once we resolve upon it, and when we do, everything about us changes. We see what we had been blind to, we undertake what we had been anxious to escape; and suddenly, the world is blown upon as in the morning of creation, and all the earth is swept as by the winds of God.

When the soul breaks forth again, it will end this time of tight-clenched hands and little hearts, and we shall know once more how deep and natural is faith in life and

God and one another. But it is not our province to await that hour as though nothing can be done until it comes. The great changes of history do not happen while men stand idly by, waiting for them. History is changed by those who decide to change it. And so is human life at every level.

Whenever, therefore, we are *willing* to awaken to the larger life that is sounding like a drum-beat through our torpor, we are *able* to do so. In that moment, we can start. And as we journey, we shall find what Whitman sang of: "life immense in passion, pulse and power"; and what Jesus meant by "life abundant."

3

What Are You Running Away From?

THERE ARE some people you meet, and some you just read about, who seem to be in a hurry not so much to get somewhere as to get away from something. They give you the impression that they are secret fugitives from a concealed pursuer. "What is it," you feel like asking them, "that you are running away from?" But you repress the question because you know at once that to reply to it would be embarrassing.

As a matter of fact, however, with a little reflection you can discover the answer for yourself. Here is a business man, let us say, very successful, very wealthy, in a hurry to give some money away. He wants to do good, and on as generous a scale as possible. Well, is there anything wrong with it? Perhaps not; nevertheless, it keeps occurring to you that generosity is not his only motive. Something is driving him. After a little further thought, you know what it is. The rich man who has turned to philanthropy is trying to leave behind him the rich man who made the money. There are things he wants to forget, to escape from, to cover over with happier memories. And he seems to be in a considerable hurry.

One is reminded of the famous stock manipulator, a financial buccaneer of the nineteenth century, who made a great deal of money at some expense to his conscience. One day, he was being driven from the railway station in a small city in New York State, and while he was some distance from his destination, a thunderstorm came on and the lightning struck a large tree just a few feet from his carriage. When the horses had been calmed down, he asked to be driven immediately to the home of the nearest minister. This was done, and when he had introduced himself, he told the story of the bolt of lightning and asked the minister what he thought about it. Had God intended the incident as a warning, deliberately directing this token of his wrath against himself, the money-maker?

The minister made some discreet inquiries, mostly financial, and replied that he thought that God was indeed angry. "What can I do about it?" asked the financier. "Well," said the minister, "there is an addition to my church that I am trying to raise some money to build; perhaps what you are intended to do is make a substantial contribution—the entire amount, possibly, that you made on the Stock Exchange yesterday." This the financier immediately did, and was glad to buy protection from the elements so cheaply. The minister, apparently, was not afraid of thunderbolts, or believed, perhaps, that God approved the mulcting of a Wall Street magnate!

We have this same feeling that someone is running away from something when we watch the careers of certain politicians. So loud are they for patriotism, so eager to expose in others alleged defects of loyalty, and yet so seldom do they work and vote for those proposals which prefer the country's benefit to selfish interests. They are in such haste to make a flurry and create a stir that you begin to wonder. What is it, you ask, about this man that awakens your suspicion? Something in his background that you cannot quite identify, something in his earlier days, something that invites your speculation, and as you

watch him, you know that this, whatever it is, is what he
is running away from.

One is reminded in all such instances of the story of
Jacob in the Old Testament, fabled founder of the twelve
tribes of Israel. He was the man who stole his brother's
birthright and had to run away from home.

He had no difficulty in working out the actual strata-
gem. Esau, his brother, was a crude man, an outdoors
man, a hunter, without spiritual sensitivity. Jacob, on the
other hand, was God's man of destiny, with refined sensi-
bilities and deeply spiritual. God was pointing at himself
and Jacob knew it! It was *he* who should have the birthright—and also his father's sacred blessing. And with his
mother's help, he got them. Then, he had to run for his
life from Esau.

Yes, but not only from Esau. Jacob also had to run from
Jacob. Not from Jacob, the man of destiny—of course not!
—but from Jacob, the deceiver and cheat.

The first night out from home, his tortured conscience
gave itself the relief of a comforting dream, a dream that
provided him with a ladder between himself and heaven.
What admirable psychology! Whoever the makers of this
ancient story were, they certainly knew—centuries before
the time—the modern psychological approach. A ladder of
wish-fulfillment! A magic ladder built for a man who, on
the basis of his present character, could never climb
anywhere without one.

So here we have it, a magic ladder up and down which
his dreams can go—effortlessly—while leaving the dead-
weight of his pursuing self behind. Furthermore, the
dream continues, God makes a covenant with Jacob, and
gives him an absolute guarantee for the future. This, also,
is of psychological interest. But let us pass on.

Let us note that even in his dream, his other self, the cheating self, crept in. That is the trouble with it: just when you think you have got rid of it, why, there it is, as evident as ever! And this other self turns the spiritual guarantee into a commercial contract. Jacob offers the Deity ten percent on his investment! God is to make Jacob thrivingly prosperous, as well as a religious man and a man of destiny, and in return, Jacob will give God ten percent. What a beautiful, reassuring dream! God provides the capital, does most of the work and takes all the risk. For that he gets ten percent! Jacob agrees to allow God to make him rich. For that he takes ninety percent!

Can we wonder that when morning came, Jacob had to go on running. And long after he had reached the haven of his Uncle Laban's homestead, he was still running— running away from himself. He plunged into ceaseless activity; he made the old ranch bloom with unheard-of prosperity, carrying everything forward by his restless, anxious, nervous energy—and all the while, running away from himself. Running and still running! running and always running! When he worked and when he prayed, when he laughed and when he wept, when he loved and when he hated, running, running, running—away from himself.

Every so often, he would catch an unwelcome glimpse of that repugnant self that he hoped he had outrun, and it would make him run faster. He caught a glimpse of it sometimes, reflected in the hard bargaining of his Uncle Laban and in the sharp practices with which he met it. He found his subtlety of comprehension, his spiritual sensitivity, compelled to serve his shifty, crafty ambition, to wait upon his greed. God's man of destiny bowed down again and again before Jacob, the cheat. It was tormenting at times, but he couldn't bring himself to face it; he just kept on running. And there was always the relief of dreaming, the solace of his spiritual fantasy.

Then, finally, he had to run away from Laban, too; for his cousins, the children of Laban, detested him, all but the two daughters, who had become his wives. And even of these he was not sure until he had inquired about their loyalty, whether it was to their father or to him. He told himself that it was Jacob, God's man of destiny, whom the household hated. But he had to run, and run fast, to make sure that it was not Jacob the shifty, Jacob the insatiable, Jacob the cheat.

Then something astounding happened. Let me say again that whoever wrote this story was a psychological genius: either that or genius was in the people who told and retold it through the many generations before it was recorded. For this is the thing that happened: Jacob ran away from Laban and found that he was running towards Esau. He was trapped. Presently, his uncle overtook him and the matters between them were settled. That, too, was a precarious moment and Jacob had to cheat very energetically; but it turned out all right.

Now, however, there was Esau. And Jacob was sore afraid. No longer could he disguise from himself what manner of man he was. Events were ruthlessly revealing it. The two selves that were Jacob had to come together and fight it out. This is what we read: "And Jacob was left alone; and there wrestled a man with him until the breaking of the day."

Now there are several elements in that story, some of which we need not, for our present purpose, be concerned with. It is the biographical significance that we are following. And from that standpoint, what happened was that Jacob fought it out with Jacob. The story says that he wrestled with the ambassador of God, but it comes to the same thing. When a man's lower self wrestles with his higher self, when his egoism wrestles with his conscience, when his craftiness and cunning fight it out with his soul, that man is indeed wrestling with the ambassador of God. That is why I say that Jacob fought it out with Jacob. His other self had caught up with him and no longer could there be evasion. Thus it was that in the morning the soul of Jacob had at last prevailed.

Is it not a familiar story?—familiar not because you have heard it before, or read it in the Bible, but because you know about it in experience.

We try to run away from ourselves. For a time, we seem to succeed—at a price! It is a rather high price, the price of breathless haste, of feverish anxiety, of ever-recurring intervals of torment. Sooner or later, the reckoning comes. The pursuing self catches up.

Let us look at this briefly, in the context of modern psychology. I am well aware that it is far more complicated than our present study will disclose; it runs all the way from minor aberrations to insanity, and from the slightest moral deviation down to the final disintegration of the personality. But let us see it in a simplified fashion for the present, so that we shall not lose our way in the complexities.

What happens is this: part of our life, because the truth about it is unwelcome to us, is dissociated from our conscious thought about ourselves. We repress it. It thereupon becomes what is called a "complex," or if it is more severe, a "neurosis," or if it is utterly severe, a "psychosis," by which our whole personality is brought to confusion and sanity itself breaks down.

But let us leave the extremes and focus our attention upon the more average case. The individual holds, shall we say, a certain standard of conduct or a certain idealism and considers himself devoted to it and loyal to its claims. He cannot think of himself as stooping below this standard, or contemplate betraying it. He associates it firmly with himself; he is *identified* with it. His pride, his self-esteem, are bound up with it. But there are other things in his life, more elemental things. There is greed, or ruthless ambition, or aggressive selfishness; or a powerful wish for self-display, or an urge to dominate, or a shabby streak of shiftiness, or even just an idle self-indulgence—any of these things or of many others. They stem from the untamed forces which life supplies from the energies of animal man.

Now what happens? The individual finds himself drawn to let these impulses loose in his life, but on the other hand, he has identified his higher self with an idealism, with a personal standard or with a lofty purpose. What does he do? All too often, he does what Jacob in the story did: he allows these impulses of his unworthy self to have their way in his life but he refuses to recognize them for what they are; he "rationalizes" whatever he does so as to make it seem as though he is living in accordance with his standard. Jacob, for example, argues himself into believing that since he is a superior person, superior particularly in spiritual sensitivity as compared with Esau, he *ought* to have the birthright and so he proceeds to get it, justifying the means by the end.

He soon convinces himself that Esau is a crude, barbaric sort of creature whose open-hearted honesty is mere stupidity. Esau, he says, has no subtlety, his character is organized on a simple plane, his virtues are like those of the beasts of the fields, thoughtless and unselfconscious. But he, Jacob, is a highly-organized personality, intellectually subtle, spiritually very sensitive; he *feels* things as Esau never feels them. "Why," thinks Jacob, "if Esau were in my place and wanted what I want, he would simply take it; it would not even appear to him as a temptation." And so on and on, until the 'rationalization' is complete and Jacob can steal without feeling himself a thief, can supplant without seeing himself a usurper, can deceive without knowing himself a cheat, can run away without having to call himself a coward. That is how it is done; and that, with our own particular problems, is how we try to do it, too.

Thus, the hateful truth about ourselves is kept disguised; we refuse to believe that *that* particular self exists at all. We dissociate it from our conscious picture of ourselves. Then what happens? We begin to take refuge in dreams and fantasies; we begin to *run* and we plunge into restless activity; the dissociated piece of our lives becomes a "complex" or a "neurosis" or whatever else somebody cares to call it.

And what does it do to us? We think we can separate ourselves from it and outdistance it but actually it stows away in our lives; yes, but not quietly and peaceably. Far from it! It begins to trouble us vaguely and "far away," then it comes closer. At the critical moment, just as we are facing the difficult event and the demanding circumstance, it stabs us in the back and we are defeated. It frustrates us, robs achievement of its glory. It lurks always in the shadows, tormenting us. It uses up most of our energy keeping it repressed; and we run, run, run, thinking to keep ahead of it.

When it closes in upon us, we rationalize more desper-

ately. I wonder if it was not at a later stage, relatively,
that Jacob thought up his extreme rationalization about
Esau having got himself born first, although at the beginning of the twin birth it was Jacob who was likely to be
the firstborn? That rather odd story certainly appears in
the narrative. Rationalization builds upon rationalization
until the whole top-heavy structure is ready to fall down.
Then we must use up all our emotional resources, trying
to maintain it. To such desperate expedients are we driven
in flying from reality, hoping against hope that we can
leave that other self behind.

Sometimes, of course, we think we are succeeding; we
believe we are beyond pursuit. But it is seldom long before we know that we are being deluded. Our situation is
similar to that of the horse at the circus—the horse that
rushes swiftly past a man with a rope. The horse must feel
that once beyond the man, he has left danger behind him
and is safe, or at least, he would feel so until experience
taught him otherwise. But it is far from the fact. For when
the horse is many yards beyond the man with the rope,
the rope swings out in a sudden rapid movement and the
horse is stopped in its tracks, lassoed.

It is the same thing that happens to the man who thinks
he has outrun his other self. The moment of danger seems
past; then, suddenly, the outreach from behind stops the
man in his tracks, perhaps in the moment of crisis or the
hour of opportunity. For no one can run fast enough to
leave himself behind.

New scenes and new circumstances will not avail in the
least. Thousands of men and women have gone all around
the earth, running away from themselves, or have settled
down in new places supposing that the old self would be
left behind. It cannot. Not without a more drastic change
than change of scene.

This futility of flight is shown, of course, not only in matters which lie clearly in the realm of conscience but in every part of life. No one can leave reality behind. A person, for instance, who refuses to relinquish youth and pretends that he has not grown older must be included in this category. Such a person, rushing hither and yon in demonstration of his juvenile interests, will show age sooner than others. He is also likely to develop anxiety, even an 'anxiety neurosis,' for his energies will be depleted by exhausting excursions into the impossible. He will be battered down by the never-ending need to keep up appearances, vainly trying to deceive both others and himself.

Meanwhile, the true rewards of frank acceptance of advance in years will all be lost. Maturity, wisdom, confidence, serenity—all these will be surrendered. And for nothing! For the aging self that is repudiated will infallibly catch up. When it does, a melancholy moment has been reached. What sadder spectacle can one conceive than that of the individual who has arrested his own growth, frustrated his natural fulfillment?

The fact is that you have to take yourself with you, always, recognized or unrecognized, freely or as a stowaway. And this is true of the whole range of life. It is true of the estimate we have of our abilities. If we hold to a flattering self-fantasy and leave our real self and its true but limited abilities neglected—or try to do so—we are condemning ourselves to a life of intermittent torture. Furthermore, the day of disclosure is always threatening.

It is clear, then, that we are dealing with a very broad principle indeed; its applications are as the sands of the seashore for multitude.

What is to be done about it? The first thing to be done is to make an act of recognition and to make it completely.

In doing this, we should know that an act of recognition is also an act of will. It is because we do not will it that we do not recognize ourselves. Socrates knew this when he counselled, many centuries ago, that before all things else a man should begin by knowing himself. Socrates knew that self-knowledge was something that a man had to will himself to achieve. He had to be *willing* to see himself—*all* of himself. It was this that Jacob had to do in the end and when he came out of the experience he was forever changed.

The change began with the recognition. When a man cheats, he should call it cheating; when he does shoddy and shabby things for shoddy and shabby reasons he should say so. When he is greedy, he should call it greed. When he is selfishly burning with ambition, he should say that selfish ambition is what he is burning with. And whatever it is, he should call it by its honest name and not try to justify it on the basis that it is something else.

He should see these things as *in him,* as part of him. In all respects, a person should make a true reckoning with himself. When he gets ready to sell out his idealism, he should say to himself, "I am about to sell out my idealism." "Oh," but you say, "if a man said that, he would be very unlikely to sell out his idealism." Yes, I know; that is why he should say it. Call wrong, wrong, and you are more than half-way to resisting it. Call an evil intention, evil, and it begins to cease to be an intention. That is why it is more than merely the clearing up of a confusion when we recognize ourselves. It is the beginning of a transformation.

The best way in the world to get a child to wash his face is to hold before him a mirror. In the same way, psychological health, moral health, spiritual health, all begin with self-recognition.

Have you noticed that the people who hated Jesus in the Gospels were the ones who did not want to make that sort of recognition? They wanted to go on thinking well of themselves just as they were, including their sins. And, of course, they wanted sin called something else. So, like ourselves, they clung to their precious "complexes" and cherished their beloved "neuroses," choosing to go through life, hunted and haunted, rather than face the truth. Indeed, it was because Jesus made the truth so unbearably plain that some of them wanted to get rid of him. And yet, for every one of them, there came a day when the self from which he fled caught up with him. It is always so. How much better, then, to turn about and face this self at once; and thereupon to make an honest reckoning. When we do that, life is no longer a furtive flight and a fugitive journey, but a full and joyous pilgrimage.

4

The Forgiveness That Comes Hardest

MOST PEOPLE learn the meaning of forgiveness from their parents, especially from the mother. The young child who has been rebuked by his mother for something he has said or done feels insecure without her approval. So, in one way or another, he seeks a reconciliation. This is his first experience of forgiveness.

Presently, owing to the influence of the father, the matter becomes more complicated. Usually, though not, of course, invariably, it seems to the child that the restraints of the father are more formidable, and this element combines with the tenderer one which relates to the mother.

In any case, from the interactive influence of the two parents upon him, the child, without really knowing why, begins to think of some actions as likely to gain approval and other actions as certain to be disapproved. But since he never succeeds in restricting himself to the approvable actions only, he finds himself from time to time in need of toleration or indulgence, or of what he learns to call forgiveness.

When he moves out from the home into a wider social environment—the playground, the school, the homes of his friends—he discovers that this attitude of approval and disapproval is encountered wherever he goes. So that it becomes implanted within himself. Some things he can do and be glad that he has done them; other things cause him unhappiness, self-criticism, remorse.

Sooner or later, he learns that this is not fortuitous; it is part of the nature of things, commanded, he is told, by God. And he thinks of God as a good deal like his father but more powerful, and yet at the same time not unlike his mother; so that the same God who condemns him for what is disapproved may also be asked to reinstate him or—as he says—forgive him.

Out of all this, the child as he grows becomes aware of what he calls his conscience, and sometimes is much perplexed by it. If his development is well regulated, his conscience will be such that his reason reinforces it; that is to say, he will consider on his own account to what extent the judgments of his conscience make sense and improve his life and its relationships, and will accept those judgments; and at the same time he will reject his guilt-feelings wherever he sees them to be something left over from his infancy and irrational.

But this is not a thing he will do easily. If his parents have been unwise, or estranged and quarrelsome, or lacking in affection, or over-indulgent, or in other ways inadequate, the grown child may suffer for it all his life. His conscience may never be wholesome. Or the same thing may happen through some defect in himself. And thus, evidently, we are discussing something that is far from simple. In some people, it works straightforwardly. These people are mature. But in other people it works quite deviously and does much harm. These people have been impeded in emotional development; no matter how bright their minds, they are *immature*.

When it comes to forgiveness, therefore, which all of us throughout our lives must both seek for ourselves and,

from time to time, concede to other people, those who
are mature manage it fairly easily but those who are
immature are constantly in difficulties with it. They are
in difficulties because their own consciences are confused,
and this confusion which exists within themselves they
project out into the lives of other people.

Let me illustrate. A few years ago, a lady came into my
office, hoping that I could help her to find her way out
of a rather tangled situation. Some injuries had been done
to her, she said, which she had freely forgiven. The people
who had done these injuries were very hateful people: she
was sure of that, but nevertheless she had forgiven them.
She was acting generously and wanted to go on acting
generously. On the surface it was a very creditable story.
The lady had done well. But if she had done well, why
was she disturbed about it? Why were there tears of anger
in her eyes? Why was she seeking help?

The truth was, of course, that she had not done well at
all. The forgiveness expressed in her behavior was not a
forgiveness that came from the heart. She hated these
people. And why did she hate them? Was it for what
they had done to her? Not really. This kind of hatred
never persists because of what other people do: it is rooted
in what one does oneself. This lady hated her relatives
and friends because of her self-hate. She could not forgive
them because she could not forgive herself.

This, after a while, was what I suggested to her. "Why
don't you forgive the person most concerned?" I asked.
"Isn't it your chief trouble that you can't forgive yourself?" And then she told me of her childhood, a very
unhappy one, and of the tortures of conscience—of a confused and sick conscience—which she had never been able
to make well. She was in part the victim of her upbring-

ing—as most such people are. But she was also to blame herself—if one may call it blame. She had fortified herself within her own resentments—resentments, however, which she had learned to repress and conceal. She was outwardly sweet and gracious; inwardly she was seething with hostility. She could not forgive herself for *being* herself, and for not being better than she was. And she represents thousands of other people—not only thousands but millions.

These people, as I have indicated, have become what they are largely through an unfortunate childhood conditioning. For that reason, they should be understood sympathetically. Yet sympathy alone will never cure them. They have to gain insight into their own invalidism; they have to understand that, in their cases, conscience is not a guide to spiritual health but only a mechanism for gaining approval. They have to know that a more wholesome state of conscience is possible. And they have to begin by forgiving themselves—which is the hardest kind of forgiveness.

Such people are often very good people—that is to say, in overt behavior. If they are cruel or intolerant, it is always in a quite disguised and very subtle way. If they do other people an injury, they always make it seem like a kindness: something generous on the surface which is nevertheless intended as a condescension, or even a humiliation. The rectitude of their outer lives conceals an inner lie.

As I have said, this is not a simple condition—or one that is easy to describe. The extent to which I have described it gives only the barest indications. Nor has it been possible to describe it even to this extent until rather recent years, for in this matter we are much indebted to modern psychology. Nevertheless, the condition itself is not new, and neither is its importance. It was this self-hatred, this self-accusing unforgiveness, that gave impulse to heresy-hunts and inquisitions, and to all the harshness perpetrated in the name of religion. It has done the same thing in the life of families. It has destroyed the harmony of human relationships of every sort.

Anyone who wishes to see what its effect was in the Victorian Era can do so by reading Samuel Butler's *Way of All Flesh.* Or if they wish to follow the matter for another generation or so, they can read *The Forsyte Saga.* Or, for a thoroughly modern and very clear and useful treatment they can go to Rabbi Liebman's *Peace of Mind,* particularly the third chapter.

There is no forgiveness—none whatever—that comes so difficult as the forgiveness wherewith we forgive ourselves. I sometimes think it might be added to the petition in the Lord's Prayer. "Forgive us our trespasses as we forgive those who trespass against us, and help us also to forgive ourselves, so that our forgiveness of others may be genuine." It is not too difficult—not usually—to forgive those who trespass against us. However deeply we resent an injury at first, after a while we are ready to forgive it. Our trouble is that it is not the injury done *to* us, but the injury we *do* that is hard to forgive. We can forgive others, in one measure or another, but we cannot forgive ourselves.

The person who has done us a wrong we are not embarrassed to meet; but the person to whom *we* have done a wrong—we cannot forgive *him* because we cannot forgive ourselves. He is a constant reminder of what we want to forget—that *we* did a wrong. So we project the wrong we did out on to him; and such is the ingenuity of our minds that we provide arguments to persuade ourselves that we did *not* do the wrong; it was the other way around: *he* did it.

But what it comes to is quite plain when we are willing to look at it. *We cannot forgive ourselves.* And the reason, of course, is that we do not want to admit that we need forgiveness. We want to justify ourselves. Not outwardly, perhaps. No, but in the last analysis. For we do not want to face ourselves as we really are.

And whether this is brought upon us by our childhood conditioning, producing in us a muddled conscience, or whether it is something that we bring about ourselves— or both, and I think that it is often both—what we are up against is that we hate ourselves. And so we project our self-hate out into the world and out towards other people.

From this—or so I increasingly think—comes more unhappiness, more sickness of soul, than from anything else in the world. It is quite frequently from self-hate that people commit suicide. But there is also a self-killing that goes on in day-to-day existence: a sort of chronic suicide. People kill off a part of their own nature—the best part— and because they do, all their relationships have something of death in them. They kill off the kindliness in other people, the natural friendliness that is offered to them, the spontaneities that make life joyous and bountiful. Wherever they go, these people, they are killers of the soul. Yet, there is nothing that they do to other people that is anything like as harmful as what they do to themselves. Human beings are not like serpents, immune to their own venom: in poisoning others, they poison themselves.

Well, what may be done about it? Rabbi Liebman, in the book I mentioned, says that "the religion of the future should take a page from the notebook of the psychotherapist." That, perhaps, is what I have been doing. If we can identify a condition, if we can truly recognize it and not disguise it, we are already gaining power over it. That is what the psychotherapist would tell us. We must gain insight. We must know ourselves as we are. We must recognize ourselves in our true character. Then, we can do something *about* ourselves. We can forgive ourselves.

Perhaps we can even begin to laugh at ourselves. We can see how comical we sometimes are, how full of tricks and stratagems, how far from the perfections we have tried to claim. And we can get used to ourselves. Instead of living with a tortured conscience, too sick to guide us, we can achieve a wholesome conscience and learn to accept its directions. We can stop being afraid of ourselves, cease using up our emotional energy trying to pretend. We can *be* ourselves, but with an honest effort to be truly better than we have been in the past. All this we can achieve, says the psychotherapist, through insight. For with insight comes humility. Not a false modesty, covering up an inordinate vanity that we do not want other people to know about. But humility: seeing ourselves for what we are and knowing what to respect in ourselves and what to put up with while we try to get the better of it.

What this humility is in ordinary ways—not heroic or dramatic ways but just in common ways—has often been illuminated for me when I have remembered an occasion, several years ago, in the state of Maine, when I was driving through a sparsely populated countryside and began to run out of gasoline. Just as I was getting desperate, I saw a gasoline pump half a mile down a hill and managed to get to it. But by this time a thunderstorm was on its way. And the old man who had been vending the gasoline took a look at the sky and hurried off into a barn. Nor could I persuade him to leave its shelter and come and sell me some gasoline—not until the storm was safely passing down the river. Then he came out of the barn. Not in the least embarrassed, he looked into the car window and with his face wrinkled up into a quizzical, whimsical sort of smile, whispered to me, "I'm not the bravest man in these parts."

Well, he wasn't. And he would have been better off if he had been a little braver. But just the same, he was no hypocrite. Nor was there anything wrong with his humility. I'm quite sure that he'll never have a neurosis—not even a complex. What he is, he is, and he had probably done the best he could about himself. If a bolt of lightning was going to hit the gasoline tank and blow up some city folks, why it was something to regret but not something to share. He was "not the bravest man in those parts." But he was *something*—he was honest and humble and he didn't hate himself.

Perhaps, at his age, he ought to have achieved a little more than that. Doubtless, he would himself have said so. But there are quite a lot of people, both older and younger than he, and with far wider opportunities, who are much below him in accomplishment. For they are not honest—not really—nor humble, and they *do* hate themselves. They pretend to forgive everybody else, but they don't; and they don't forgive the world they live in, or the God who made it. They don't forgive anyone or anything—not really—because they can't forgive themselves.

All this, as we said a moment ago, is pointed up for us by modern psychotherapy. Yes, but not alone by that. Valid insights are never altogether new. And this one isn't.

For what does this story mean: two men went up to the
Temple to pray, one a Pharisee, the other a publican. And
the Pharisee lifted up his voice and said, "God, I thank
thee that I am not as other men. I lead an upright life. I
keep the commandments, pay my bills, give a little to
charity, never cheat, never gamble, never curse, never
drink. I am respectable . . . and certainly not like this
publican here." And the publican beat his hands on his
breast, not daring to raise up his eyes unto heaven, and
cried, "God be merciful to me a sinner!" Which of these
two, asked the Man from Nazareth, went down justified?

Let us take another look at them, these two. A Pharisee
—who hated himself so much that he didn't dare to take
his mind off his piety. "O God," something deep inside
him was saying, "I hate the world, I hate the people in it,
I hate you and I hate myself." But he stifled it by crying
out his virtues that much the louder. Otherwise, his prayer
would have been something like this: "O God, I thank
thee that I am not as other men, extortioners, unjust, adul-
terers—or even as this publican. (I hate him! I hate this
publican! He makes me see what I am really like, just as
full of temptations as he is—and worse, because I'm cold
and cruel and he isn't.) O God, I fast twice in the week,
I give tithes of all I get. (Why aren't you grateful, God?
Listen! I fast! I do without things! I give away my money!
Why aren't you grateful, God? I hate you. I hate you for
letting me seem so feeble, so stuffy, so pallid, so lifeless,
while I do all this for *you!*) O God, I keep the sabbath, I
set a good example, I follow the ritual. I'm not like other
men. I'm righteous. (Yes, righteous! I hate other men. I
daren't let myself know how much I'm like them. I'm a
hypocrite. But this, God, is something you mustn't know—
you mustn't know that *I* can't forgive *you*: that I can't

forgive you for creating me the way I am, to live in the world the way it is. And for all this I'm full of poison and hatred and *I can't forgive myself.*")

That, I think, is how it really was when the two men went up to the Temple to pray. And the other man just said, "Be merciful, O God. (I *have* loved the world, I have loved its people, I have loved myself—too much! And I love you. If it's blasphemy for one like me to say it, I can't help it. God, I think you are different from the stories they tell about you. God, I don't think you're like they say you are at all. I think you know that I've not done very well; and it's possible that I may not do much better.) Be merciful! (I'll do the best I can with myself. But it won't be very good. And yet I won't be able to keep on being miserable about it. Although I don't deserve to be, I'm liable to be happy. I don't quite know what to make of myself— but I have no other self. This is me and all there is of me. You had it in mind to make me something more than this. I know, God. I've let you down. But I shall have to forgive myself. I want to go away from here cleansed. I want *you* to forgive me.) Be merciful. . . ." That's how it was when two men went up to the Temple to pray.

And, said Jesus, it was the publican who went home justified. It was he who found peace of mind. What wonderful things would happen to this weary world if its heartsick people should find the same secret.

5

A Little Matter of Conscience

CONSCIENCE has never been popular. Even when people believed in its authority and tried to be obedient to it, they seldom really liked it. Either it prevented them from doing what they wanted, or disturbed them when they went ahead in spite of it. They said of it that it "gnawed at them." They felt that Shakespeare had hit the mark precisely with his phrase, "the worm of conscience." That is what it seemed to be: something that kept burrowing into their happiness and undermining it.

With the advent of the new psychology, however, conscience began to seem less fearsome. It was not a separate entity, implanted in the soul; it was the product of "conditioning." But was this *all* it was, or was there something definite to start with that could be conditioned? Montaigne had said, as long ago as 1580, that "the laws of conscience, though we ascribe them to nature, actually come from custom." Much the same viewpoint was held by Schopenhauer, and was given complete expression by Nietzsche. It was the latter who said that "the sting of conscience, like the gnawing of a dog at a bone, is mere foolishness." And he went on to say that it is possible to train the conscience so that it kisses instead of bites. A bad conscience, he declared, is nothing but "a kind of illness." And there were others who thought the same.

Freud approached the question of conscience as a specialist in mental aberration, a clinical physician. It gave people "guilt feelings" which had no basis in reality but nonetheless imprisoned them. This aspect of conscience, thought Freud, should be understood more scientifically and he set out to understand it. With the diligence that was characteristic of him, he went right back to the primitive and began to trace the molding of conscience through the growth of custom. Religion, he discovered, operating through fear, imposed the customs of the tribe not only externally, by force of public opinion, but also internally, by shaping the minds of its victims to a patternized tradition. They were thus intimidated from without and terrorized within, both at the same time.

Thus regarded, Freud concluded, conscience is seen to be a system of attitudes conditioned by tradition. As for its sanction, it was chiefly superstition. A better understanding would get rid of guilt feelings and permit the development of what he called the "super-ego" which could be rationally trained. Modern psychologists in many cases have equated conscience with the super-ego. In their *Handbook of Psychiatry*, Overholser and Richmond tell us that conscience or the "super-ego" "develops out of the prohibitions, the commands and the teachings of parents and teachers. At first the child is wholly dependent upon them to guide his actions; but gradually he sets up within himself standards of what to do or not to do, of what is right and wrong." This, however, only takes place where development is normal and healthy. There are people who "cling to the teachings of their parents and cannot move with the times." These are the people who are preyed upon by guilt feelings and whose consciences are morbid and irrational.

Some psychologists, however, have gone to extremes in condemning conscience, and so have some psychiatrists.

It has been much easier for psychology to understand the guilt feelings produced by the wrong kinds of religion than to understand those which are caused by resistance to genuine morality. In many cases, the psychiatrist who is consulted by a patient who is morally confused is himself as badly off as his patient, though perhaps less troubled by it: he has, that is to say, no moral standards that he deeply believes in and no spiritual faith which could support such standards. Thus, the most he can do is help his patient to get rid of irrational restraints (and sometimes restraints which are not irrational) without being able to tell him what a well adjusted conscience would approve. This is not altogether his fault, but merely means that in solving the problems of faith and morals for the drifting humanity of the modern age, he is no wiser than others.

These more extreme psychologists would do well to consider as a starting-point what Darwin had to say about conscience in *The Descent of Man.* "Any animal whatever," says Darwin, "endowed with well-marked social instincts, the parental and filial affections being here included, would inevitably acquire a moral sense or conscience, as soon as its intellectual powers had become as well, or nearly as well, developed as in man."

Darwin, the experienced and accurate observer, takes us at once to the heart of the matter. Provided an animal must get along with other animals, provided it has known protective care from its own species, and provided it begins to have mentality so that it can reflect upon its own behavior, it will distinguish between kinds and levels of behavior. Having known kindness, it will feel sympathy, and this will invite it to be compassionate rather than cruel. If it declines this invitation and elects to be cruel, the memory of the kindness it has itself received reproaches it. And so with everything else.

It is a matter of motivation, and proceeds from what the animal is as an emotional entity. It may be rational or irrational, according to the basis upon which it is judged, but in any case, since a choice exists as to whether a particular motive is followed or repelled, the animal is deciding between better and worse, between what it can approve and what it must disapprove, and so we come, as Darwin said we must, to the dawning of the moral sense or conscience, and this is the way we must come to it in man.

Immanuel Kant, one of the greatest of the classical philosophers, has been sharply criticized for saying that conscience is instinctive. "It is not a mere faculty," he said: "it is an instinct." We do not use the word *instinct* today as he did in the eighteenth century, but if we allow for this difference, partly in concept and partly in vocabulary, we see that Kant is choosing the word that gives his meaning greatest emphasis; like Darwin, he is insisting that conscience is a basic element of human nature. It may be conditioned in any of a number of ways, both wholesome and unhealthy, but it cannot be eradicated. It is there because we need it, because we cannot get along without it, because it makes it possible for human societies to exist and for human individuals to find their way to what they really want without getting lost in blindness and confusion.

I shall labor this point a little, because, as I said at the beginning, conscience nowadays is regarded rather skeptically. One of the consequences of this, or so I think, is the low level to which we have fallen in standards of behavior in public office and in positions of trust. The same is true, and few will doubt it, in the lives of individuals.

Conscience should be counted out, we are told. That is

what a psychiatrist—one of the extreme kind—said to me over the telephone, a little while ago. He was not representative of the best in his profession, the thoughtful, forbearing and often very humble men who are constantly seeking deeper insight into the dark recesses of human life. He was very sure of himself, which is a fatal defect in a psychiatrist—as it is in a minister, or in almost anyone else. What had happened was that one of his patients had insisted upon seeing me to discover whether I thought that he was moving along right lines under the guidance of this psychiatrist. He was a highly cultivated, very sensitive person, much concerned with religion.

I told him that it would be improper and perhaps harmful for me to talk with him without first getting the views of his psychiatrist. He therefore gave me permission to telephone the doctor, which I did from another room, and I began by saying that I disliked to proceed with the interview with this man without hearing what the psychiatrist thought of it, or anything else he might wish to tell me. I have frequently cooperated with psychiatrists, sometimes on my initiative, sometimes on theirs, and have also, when it seemed wisest, suggested to a parishioner or patient that he seek no interviews for the time being other than with the psychiatrist. I was therefore much astonished at hearing over the telephone, even before I had finished introducing the matter, a noisy blast of vituperation. The world will never be any good, this psychiatrist told me, until religion and conscience are made an end of and ministers are all numbered with the unemployed. I was rather abashed at this somewhat sweeping condemnation, although I did have the presence of mind to suggest to the doctor that he would benefit, perhaps, from seeing a really good psychiatrist.

It must not be supposed from the foregoing—or from anything in these paragraphs—that I am attacking the newer methods in psychology. On the contrary, I firmly support them, and I regard psychiatrists as highly useful and important people. What I am concerned with is the correction of an emphasis—sometimes it is emphasis and sometimes downright error—the opinion, namely, that conscience in itself is damaging to mental health. Psychiatrists like the doctor I have quoted, who maintain this error, must be counted dangerous to their patients. For conscience *cannot* be eradicated, even if that is our wish; and it *should not* be eradicated because it is indispensable both to the individual and to society; what is often necessary is that it be *re-educated*.

I am not appealing—and this should be noted—to theological authority. I am appealing to nothing but experience and reason. Let us appeal to them a little further. Let us, for the purposes of illustration, consider a lower form of life than man. The social insects, such as bees and ants, have their lives regulated for them by instinctive patterns of behavior. They react to conditions without the intervention of thought. No matter how complex their behavior, it is almost automatic and mechanical.

Suppose, however, that in some way the impulse to behave in this fashion were removed. No alternative would be available. The life of the bee-hive or the ant-hill would fall into confusion. The colony could not survive. But let us suppose something less than this. Let us suppose that by some magic, the equivalent of a doubt were introduced into the colony so that every member of the bee-hive or the ant-hill was induced to stop and question the course of action which previously had been instinctive. This, too, would be disruptive to the colony. Bees and ants are so constituted that they have to obey the laws of their own nature.

Now, when we leave the insect world and come to human society, we see at once that natural laws at the human level are very different. Nevertheless, they exist. If we think that we have left the realm of natural law behind us, we are grievously mistaken. The fact is that human societies can only endure if the people who compose them act for the welfare of the society, and to a great extent this must be voluntary. If there is no public spirit, no cooperativeness, no allegiance to high standards of honesty, integrity and responsibility, the society will decay and after a while perish. This is because the laws of human societies are natural laws, which, at the human level, require these things.

In the same way, if individuals within a human society become inconsiderate of the claims of others, ruthless, selfish, callous, deceitful, irresponsible, all in the service of narrowly conceived ends, these individuals will not only damage the society, they will corrupt and in the end disintegrate their own humanity. Meanwhile, they will have no peace of mind, no inner repose, no confidence, no self-esteem. Their satisfaction in life, no matter what they may pretend, will steadily diminish. They will become restless, unhappy, discontented, and—as we like to say—neurotic. These people cannot be helped by stifling their consciences; conscience must be free and active. No one can restore the morally sick to health by diagnosing their guilt as "guilt feelings." What they need to be cured of is their actual guilt!

By natural law, the natural law at the human level, the only way that human individuals or human societies can achieve a full, secure or happy life is by preferring good over evil, the better against the worse, and by doing this both because it is rational and because they are responsive to the claims of an insistent, wholesome conscience.

Conscience should certainly be rational; it should withstand, that is to say, the tests of reason and intelligence to the full extent that these apply. Moreover, the extent of rational application should constantly be widened. Nevertheless, reason alone is not enough. An entirely rational society has never been attained. Complete reliance upon attempted rationality to the exclusion of other elements in human nature has always issued in disaster. It was this trend in Germany, which, in the name of science itself, ended with death chambers and genocide and all the horror of so-called scientific experiments on human beings. Repugnance to cruelty is emotional, not necessarily rational. It is true that a rational case can be made out for condemning cruelty, but it is also true that rational answers can be given which appear to refute it. The men in the Kremlin were sure that they were rational when they allowed millions to be starved in the Ukraine for the welfare—they claimed—of the future communist society. They were no less certain when they decreed the "purge" of 1937. It is not sufficient, and it cannot be sufficient, to have recourse only to reason, indispensable as reason may otherwise be. There must be emotion—educated emotion— which, when developed in appropriate ways, inspires correct behavior. In other words, there must be conscience.

That was what Darwin was so quick to see—and he was a biologist, let us remember, not a theologian or a moralist. "Any animal whatever," he declared, "endowed with well-marked social instincts, the parental and filial affections being here included, would inevitably acquire a moral sense or conscience, as soon as its intellectual powers had become as well, or nearly as well, developed as in man." What we should notice, now, in this quotation, against the background of our earlier discussion, is that Darwin sees conscience as composed of two essentials: first, mentality, developed as it is in man, and second, emotion, such as is found in parental and filial affection. It is from these two affections—the parental and filial—that other affections take their rise: sympathy, the feeling of responsibility, compassion, love. Where you have this power of affection, this highly developed emotion, says Darwin, and where you also have mentality, intellectual power, you will thereupon have moral sense, or conscience.

To this, however, will be brought a new objection. If Darwin is right, the modern skeptic will protest, must we not admit that it is precisely in this area, the area of parental and filial affection, that so much goes wrong. That's where you get "momism," and oedipus and electra complexes, and guilt feelings through the fear of offending the father-image, or of being reproached by the mother-image. Surely, this is where the damage is done, the damage that causes all the trouble with conscience, the damage that so worried Freud.

The answer is very simple. A hand can be clenched into a fist, a brain can be used to contrive evil, a heart can be filled with malice, but this does not mean that we can do without hands and brains and hearts. It only means that we must learn to use them properly. Because love can become a bondage, it is not therefore something bad, to be rejected. It should be better managed, better educated. Because parents are often unwise, doing emotional harm to their children, it is not therefore desirable to abolish parenthood: what is necessary is to improve it. The same is true of conscience. If conscience is unwholesome, the

thing to do is cleanse it, get it out where sunlight can
shine into it, try to make it healthy. For conscience can
change and grow with enlightenment—and it should. But
to get along without it is impossible, unless we are willing
to invite disaster.

I think this must be better understood. It is becoming
urgent that we understand it. Our public life is starved
for want of conscience—of active, healthy conscience,
sharply sensitive to good and bad, and quickly discerning
between right and wrong. It is the torpor of conscience
that has permitted our political corruption. It is disbelief
in conscience that has misled so many and made them
faithless in positions of trust. It is the same with private
lives; they, too, are starved for want of conscience. Indeed,
public evils begin with what goes wrong in private lives.
Officials are first of all persons, individuals. Betrayals are
never impersonal; they are deeds done by people.

Something must happen—it is vital to us—to regenerate
our national life. We need it at every level. Great Americans have always believed in conscience. "Labor to keep
alive," said Washington, "that little spark of celestial fire
called conscience." "The moral sense, or conscience," said
Jefferson, "is as much a part of a man as his leg or arm."
"I desire so to conduct the affairs of this administration,"
said Lincoln, in 1864, "that if at the end, when I come to
lay down the reins of power, I have lost every other
friend on earth, I shall at least have one friend left, and
that friend shall be down inside of me."

These are the men, and these the principles, that gave
us national greatness. All lesser views can only bemean
and undermine us. It is time to believe, and to believe
heartily, in the supremacy of conscience. The new knowledge that has affected traditional beliefs in so many ways

has not dissolved the grounds of this belief; nor will it. We can discount, and heavily, the chatter of the cynics who look down their noses at the claims of conscience. Most of those noses have lost the sense of smell. Otherwise, they would detect the odor of corruption, and this might have some impact on the humbug that they call advanced opinion.

As for the more extreme psychologists, they should broaden their basis of judgment. They should distinguish more sharply and with less fear of being 'moralistic' between guilt and 'guilt feelings'; and between neurosis and sin. The psychologists are better than the rest of us in dealing with neuroses, but the most pitiful spectacle to be seen anywhere is a psychologist out of his depth in sin.

Well, what can we do about it? Some one asked me that question not long since, in the context of his own difficulties. "What can I do?" he demanded. "I've tried everything. I'm diagnosed to death. I'm analyzed down to my primordial elements. I'm at the end of my rope. Do you think it would be of any use if I tried will power?"

"There's a case history," I answered, "that sheds a little light on your situation, especially the matter of will power. There was once a younger son, spoiled by his father, who asked for his inheritance beforehand, obtained it, turned it into cash, and went away to 'a far country.' There he had a lively time with what in those days was called riotous living. As occasion warranted, he took 'the cure,' recovered his health, and then went back to his rioting. Everybody was very sympathetic to him. He was the life of the party.

Finally, however, his money gave out, and at the same time, oddly enough, so did his friends, and he ended up feeding swine. It was while he was engaged in this reflective occupation that he became aware of his conscience. 'I have sinned,' he said. It was a word he had ceased to use. But as soon as he heard himself say it, he felt better; it had a good, plain, straightforward sound to it.

"Then, it occurred to him that if he was ever to get out of his predicament, it would have to be by standing up, beginning to walk, and going on walking until he got where he wanted to go, which, in his case, was his father's house, his home. In other words, there was nothing left but will power.

"So he said to himself, 'I will arise.' That was the beginning of his cure. His diagnosis was concluded when he said that he had sinned. The therapy began when he got upon his feet. There was no one to pull him up, and for that matter, no one to keep him down. So he got up by himself: that is to say, by will power. As a result, he eventually reached home, his difficulties mainly behind him.

"It is a fascinating case history," I heard myself remarking. "Full of most excellent psychology. In fact, if you don't mind it's being rather ancient, it's one of the best case histories on record. After all, the therapist who compiled it has been held in high esteem. Some of us think he has never been equalled."

After the interview, I continued to think of this well known story—the Parable of the Prodigal Son—and once again, as many times before, I felt the depth and power of its insight. It was when conscience reasserted itself that the cure began. Shall it be different with ourselves? It is a neurotic age, we are told, and none of us are unaffected. Oh, that we could all stretch out on the psychiatric couch, and while a patient father-substitute was listening—or we

hoped so—spill out the doleful story of our woes! Alas for
our too tender egos! Alas for our schizoid civilization!
Alas for our faded dreams and disillusioned wishful thinking! Alas for the whole wretched business—and especially,
alas for us!

Is this the picture? The final picture? Or can we break
out from this plush-lined prison of self-pity? Can we say,
quite simply and plainly, that we keep doing wrong when
we know we should do right, and that therefore we are
sinners? Shall we allow conscience to take its proper place
in life? And expect something of will power? Surely, it is
time we made a reckoning. That which we have been ne-
glecting is swiftly catching up with us, the choice between good and evil which for far too long we have
counted trivial—a little matter of conscience. It is time we
faced up to it. Events won't wait.

6

Seeking, Perchance, Yourself?

IN ALL THE WORLD of living things, nothing is more restless than the roving glance of human eyes. Even the prolonged and peering gaze moves constantly within itself
and is never really still. For the true meaning of sight is
not seeing but seeking. Although the outside world reflects itself, scene by scene, detailed and entire, within
the retina, that is not how we see it. To such exact
fidelity, we bring no comprehension. We see, not what
vision so faithfully supplies, but what we are looking for.
We pick out from the scene whatever shapes itself to our
own unquiet interest. We re-arrange the fragments to fit
a moving mosaic of our own assembling. We select from
what we see the features that engage our own particular
attention. For however wide we open our eyes, we can
see nothing that does not belong in one way or another
to what we are seeking.

Suppose someone enters a room into which he has
never been before. Do his eyes see everything in the
room? If he is an interior decorator, he sees the quality
and arrangement of the furniture; if he is a musician, he
sees the piano and the record albums in the phonograph
cabinet; if he is a scholar, he sees the books in the book-
shelves. And so on. Perhaps a lonely person would notice
most of all that the room looked "lived in," the scene of
family and social life.

Towards the end of last century, my maternal grand-

father, who lived in North Wales, took a trip to the home
of his brother in London. As evening fell, he wandered
out into the streets to see the sights. After a half-hour or
so, he turned to my grand-uncle and said, "Where are
they all going, these people? What are they all looking
for?" And inasmuch as no satisfactory answer could be
given, he took the train home the next day, having seen
enough of London.

Now, he did not do this because he was a limited person, unable to transcend rustic interests. In his own way,
he was something of a philosopher. The unusual thing
about him was his directness of decision; whatever he
resolved upon he forthwith did, provided he believed
that it was right. And when he couldn't discover what the
people of a great city were all looking for, he felt that
something was missing that he could not do without, and
went home to rediscover it.

Well, what *were* they looking for? What are they looking for today? Go into any great city and you will see
what my grandfather saw, millions of restless eyes, all
looking for something. The glance is wandering and
casual, but ready to be arrested at any moment, as soon as
what is sought seems likely to be found—even, in fact, if
there appears the slightest hope of finding it. Each of us
has seen this casual glance steady itself and become a
look of recognition, and this happens with strangers as
well as between friends.

For example, the eyes of pickets, in depression times,
focussing upon the faces of the customers who pass into
the store. Calculation, resignation, patient hate. Have you
ever looked observantly at the eyes of the store girl who
serves the prosperous patroness? Admiration, envy, cool
appraisal—and perhaps disdain. Or have you ever noticed

the eyes of the patroness when for a swift instant she reveals awareness of what is passing in the mind of the girl? Disconcertment, irritation, reassertion of composure. Have you ever seen natural enemies recognize each other in the interchange of a sidelong glance? Strangers, yet full of latent antipathy from causes they do not stop to understand! You can see all this and more in an afternoon's walk in any great city, London, Vienna, Tokyo, New York.

You can also see the happier sorts of recognition, the eyes that brighten, be it ever so little, when they find a kindly gaze—or even twinkle when they don't; you can see potential friendliness, the recognition of goodwill by goodwill, the glance which says, "If we happened to be friends we would be *good* friends," or "You and I respect each other, standing, no doubt, for about the same things." You can see all this and more in the recognitions, the casual, transient, fleeting, recognitions of strangers, given and at once forgotten. And of course, it is always present in the recognition of friends—and in those who pass for friends. Notice the eyes in that first instant of encounter before there is time to veil them; you will know, then, how they *really* feel about each other and what there is of friendship in their hearts.

It is all testimony to this fact of seeking—the endless seeking of human eyes. Seeking for what? What is it that each human entity, each individuality, is seeking for? It is seeking for what belongs to itself, and the search is as big or as small as the soul behind it and as varied as the colors of a life!

For the present, however, I want to take up just one aspect of this quest. I want to suggest that in our seeking we are not only looking for what enhances our selfhood, for what we can absorb into our lives, but that we are actually looking for *ourselves*. I do not exclude the fact that we seek also beyond ourselves; I do not forget that sometimes we enter genuinely and unselfishly into the lives of others; but I believe that in all this seeking we are looking also for ourselves. It is that, for the moment, that I wish to emphasize, both for its own sake and for the sake of where it leads.

Let us suppose that some spring morning, you climb a mountain and look out upon the world as it awakens to new life. Your mood deepens and you begin to wonder. What are you wondering about? About the world and the mystery of it? About life, its sweetness and bitterness? About the winds that carry winter away and the slow warmth which resurrects a frozen world? About beauty and the songs it makes? About the majesty and meaning of it all? About beginnings and endings, origins and destinies? About all you know that cannot be true, and all you feel that must be true?

Yes, but what are the questions to which it will lead? "What am *I*?" "What am I here for?" "Where am I going?" "How is it that I can see a whole world of life and feel it live and love it, and yet be so inconsequential, so full of little days and nights, so much a creature of this crawling earth, so distant from the sweep and wholeness of the sky? What am I? And what is it that I *almost* am and never quite become?" In these questions and a hundred others like them you are in quest of whatever is real in anything, but most of all, of whatever is real in yourself.

But let us come down from the mountain. Most of our lives are lived in valleys or on plains. Last week, we will say, you had a frustrating experience. It was a situation that you could not handle. It was an appeal for help and you could not meet it. It was a struggle to achieve something but you did not achieve it. You were explaining something to somebody and you did not explain it. The explanation got mixed up with something else; you could not find the proper words. In any case, it was a frustrating experience. And now that you stop to think about it, *you* were not quite there. *Something* of you was there but *you* were not there. Somehow, you, yourself, the essential you, slipped edgewise out of the situation; in fact, you, yourself, were never quite in it.

What exactly happened? It seems to be true, exasperatingly true, that you cannot get the whole of yourself into any situation; if you could, you could manage things differently; but, apparently, you cannot. There seems to be something disorganized right at the center of your life and it prevents your final self, your real and inner self, from concentrating its powers. You knew about it afterwards, but it seems to be a knowledge which follows and never precedes—an insight which cannot operate efficiently, a comprehension which is real but helpless. As you stop to think about it, what do you recollect? You were trying to meet a situation—yes, but more than that, in dealing with the situation you were trying to find yourself. And you did not meet the situation because you did not find yourself.

What is it that we look for in other people? Something of new interest? Some outlet for our sociability? Yes, undoubtedly. But beyond this, something more. What is it that sometimes makes us so hopeful of a new friendship? Or which repeatedly renews an old one? What are we looking for in our friends? We are looking for *ourselves!* We are hoping that the new friends will bring us the self

we seek, or that the old ones will yet reveal it to us; that
something will be said that in the saying of it makes us
more acquainted with ourselves—if only for a moment. Of
course, this sometimes really happens; and for a little
while, at least, we *are* ourselves.

But what about those other people, the people we
meet and do *not* like? What is it that we do not like? It
may be, of course, something quite external to us. But far
more likely it is not. Very frequently, what we most intensely dislike in other people is what we are afraid of
in ourselves. Otherwise, we would be less bothered by it.
But if it makes us angry and our minds dwell upon it,
then it is certain to be something which has to do with
ourselves.

For it is always likely that the sins we most self-
righteously denounce are those which powerfully attract
us. No doubt, such generalizations should be made with
caution, and that is how I mean to make them. Let them
be tested—but candidly—in every instance. Let us notice,
for example, how often the gossips who make life miserable for the hot-blooded are not wanting in carnal ap-
petite themselves. Or if they are, they secretly wish that
they were not. They condemn in others what they fear
or resent in themselves. Truly, there is not much to choose
between a salacious gossip and her victims. Nor is a prig
much better than a profligate. Virtue is not safe with
either.

But we need not stop for illustrations. We should always suspect—and if we were honest we always would—
that whatever angers us persistently in other people may
reveal some useful truth about ourselves. Perhaps the
other person represents to us what it is we do not wish to
face, something with which we have refused to reckon,
something that is thwarting our lives.

Or again, what is it that we fail to find in other people which leaves us disappointed? Is it something that is not there? Perhaps. But perhaps not. There is a great deal of mathematics in Einstein but I could spend a whole day with him and never get any of it out. The fault would not be Einstein's. What you can get from other people is largely measured by what you have, yourself.

We can see this best by reversing the emphasis and noticing how little other people sometimes get from us. When you meet one man you think only of the chance of telling him the latest funny story, but with another you are ready to talk of things which are sacred to you. Is it not a fact that different people find you in many ways a different person? The same is true of other people when they deal with *you*. The man whom you find a bore may be absorbingly interesting to somebody else. Carry this thought a little farther and it begins to be clear that we often fail to find some particular quality in another person because we are incapable of responding to it. Because, in fact, we cannot find much more than has come alive in ourselves.

When I have tried to help people whose lives have become unhappy, I have often had to think a good deal of what is meant by that much-abused word, incompatibility. Not that I think that incompatibility is always an excuse; often, it is real. But what *is* it that is real? A man says he is incompatible with his work, or with his wife, or with the world. There are some people who even see the universe as incompatible and complain about it to God. They don't like to say so but they find God incompatible, too. Well, as I have indicated, I think there is no doubt about incompatibility being real. Sometimes a man truly *is* incompatible with someone or something else. But what about a man being incompatible with himself?

What about his way of life being incompatible with the self he is seeking? The world may be demanding from him a strong and disciplined self and he has a need for such a self: that is partly what his search should bring him. But he does not want to pay the price of it. He seeks a complete self because he cannot help it, but whenever he is in danger of finding it, he evades it. And so somebody else who reveals this to him, he finds to be incompatible, for this somebody is challenging him to become his own master.

Self-mastery is not easy; no one can obtain it without paying the price. But there is also a price to be paid for *not* obtaining it: the price of unending frustration, of being only partly alive. Sometimes, I think our modern way of life is so heavy with substitutes for living that this alone weighs us down and keeps us earthlings. When I think of this there runs through my mind a verse of Edwin Arlington Robinson's:

> Think you to tread forever down
> The merciless old verities?
> And are you never to have eyes
> To see the world for what it is?
>
> Are you to pay for what you have
> With all you are? . . .

That is it! To pay for what you have with all you are! And not only to pay for material possessions in that way, but for possessing things of the mind and heart. To keep the unworthy and the mean, the self-inflating and the compromises which dissolve the joy of honest thought— we can pay for things like these with all we are. They can separate us from ourselves. That is the saddest divorce of all—the divorce of a man from himself, so that he must go on seeking what he has condemned himself never to find. To save his life, he has lost the power of living. To gain his little world, he has lost his soul.

We come back here to something so old that whenever it is freshly realized, it is as though it were original and new. Diogenes went out through the world seeking an honest man. Who was Diogenes looking for except Diogenes? You and I look through the world for hope and idealism. Where shall we find them if we do not find them in ourselves? We look for kindness. We look for compassion. We look for understanding and for love. We shall never find them where we do not take them. They are in the world when they are in ourselves. For the world will never be much greater than our own hearts.

Sometime ago, a young lady I have known almost since she was a baby wrote me a letter to tell me of her engagement; she was so full of the happiness of it that her letter was almost a song of joy. Then at the end, she had a moment of misgiving about my sympathy and wondered whether I would think that what she had written was rather silly. So she said, "It is a surprising thought to me, but I suppose all the rest of the world of sensible people think that L—(mentioning the young man's name) is just an ordinary nice young man, pleasant and rather handsome. It's amazing, but I suppose that this is what they think!" And I wrote her back and told her that although I was growing older, by the grace of God I didn't yet belong to "the world of sensible people" who thought such things as that, and I hoped I never would; that I was just as full of the joy of wonder as when I invented fabulous stories for her in her childhood; and that she need not bother about sensible people. I told her that she was quite

right: the rest of the world did not know this young man
at all. I told her that no young man beloved is ever an
ordinary young man; that every time two people really
loved each other the world began all over again; and that
always, the world is what our own hearts take to it; that
the love we carry with us makes all loveliness come true.
And if you think I told her any lies, whoever you are,
you have grown older than you needed to, and ought to
be ashamed.

All love is revelation. It reveals wonder and beauty in
all the world and it leads the lover to find himself. What
is it that men find in great exemplars if it be not their
own ultimate selves? The selves they yearn to be and are
not, except in aspiration. They listen to the prophets and
hear the voice of their own conscience; they consider
heroic lives and know that if they had not missed their
way such living might have been their own.

So is it always. So is it when a man goes seeking God
in the world of meaning and of mystery. Is God in the
beauty of the earth and sky? He is, if you take him there.
Is the spirit of God in the world of man? Yes, if you
carry it with you. But you will find God nowhere that you
do not take him any more than you will find your own
best self.

7

The Lives We Almost Live

ONE OF THE saddest things in the world, when you come to think of it, is that so many people frustrate their own lives. They do not say what they think, do what they want, or live as they wish. I do not mean by this that the world would be happier if all restraints were removed and everybody thought aloud, acted without regard for consequences and lived in a state of perpetual anarchy.

What I have in mind is that people suppress, not only the worst of their thoughts but the best; not a day passes but multitudes, everywhere on the face of the earth, in places high and low, near and remote, think more honestly than they speak and discern more justly than they are willing to admit; but they are intimidated by habits of hypocrisy and by the threat of finding themselves exposed to the antagonism of those who fear to lose the shelter of time-honored insincerities.

When it happens that truth is being distorted in a conversation, or justice is being ingeniously misconstrued, all in terms of specious popular assumptions or for the sake of some customary cherished prejudice, and when a bold and honest thought presents itself at the threshold of some one's mind and he rejects it, I say that this is one of the saddest things in the world because that person has stifled a part of his own life, has refused to be really himself, has sinned against his soul.

Equally sad is the fact that so many people do not do

what they want. I am not thinking of sudden impulse, which quite obviously must often be restrained. I am lamenting the frustration by which entire lives are kept imprisoned, and the surrender to drift and circumstance that dooms a majority of the world's population to personal disappointment and defeat. It takes courage to do what you want—to do, that is, what your deepest insights and your most deliberate judgment indicate. And for lack of this courage, most people come to the end of their days without ever really doing what they want.

We see this, of course, at many levels. It seems probable, for instance, that only a minority ever succeed in following the occupation they prefer. To some extent this is caused by factors that could not have been controlled. Perhaps the right kind of training was never possible; perhaps the immediate need to support other people was paramount; perhaps the necessary talent was missing. All these situations, and many others like them, should be understood with sympathy. It takes courage to *deny* oneself an ambition as well as to fulfill one. But nonetheless, when we have allowed for all this, it still remains true that a vast number of people are doing something they never really wanted to do because they surrendered to other people's opinions, or to the desire for money, or because they merely took the easiest way and missed their opportunity.

All this extends itself, however, beyond the occupation by which a person gains a livelihood. It may change the entire direction of development. It may rob a life, not only of a wished-for vocation, or of a precious avocation, but of its whole significance.

I remember a particularly striking, though rather whimsical illustration of this in Moss Hart and George S.

Kaufman's play, "You Can't Take It With You." The central character in the play, Grandpa Vanderhof, is an unusually relaxed but very vivid personality whose philosophy is to do what you really want to do, though with a full measure of kindness and consideration for others. He is confronting Mr. Kirby, a successful Wall Street magnate, who has allowed his business interests to pervade his entire life until he has become incapable of doing anything whatever that might be called spontaneous—indeed, he is as stiff and formal as an annual statement of assets and liabilities. And he doesn't want his son to marry into the bohemian Vanderhof family: he wants his son to be a junior version of himself—which the young man firmly but affectionately resists.

And so, Grandpa inquires of Mr. Kirby what all his living for business got him? Same kind of mail every morning, same kind of deals, same kind of meetings, same dinners at night, same indigestion. Where did the fun come in? Ought there not to have been something *more?* Mr. Kirby must have wanted more than that when he started out. "We haven't got too much time, you know—any of us."

Kirby asks Grandpa what he expects him to do—live as *he* does? "Well," replies Grandpa, "I have a lot of fun. Time enough for everything—read, talk, visit the zoo now and then, practice my darts, even have time to notice when spring comes around . . . And I haven't taken bicarbonate of soda in thirty-five years. What's wrong with that?"

And while Mr. Kirby is trying to tell Grandpa Vanderhof what he thinks is wrong with it, his son, Kirby, Jr., breaks in and insists upon relating how Father Kirby rebelled against *his* father and, at fourteen years of age,

wanted to be in a circus; then, when that was out of the
question, at eighteen years of age, tried to become a
saxophone player. Kirby pooh-poohs all this, but what he
can't pooh-pooh is that he still keeps a saxophone hidden
in the back of his clothes closet. Hearing this, Grandpa
Vanderhof wrinkles up his kindly old face in the most
satisfied of smiles and looks gently over his spectacles at
Mr. Kirby until the poor, discomfited gentleman shrugs
his shoulders and gives up.

Mr. Kirby had done what the world wanted, not what
he wanted himself; the rebellion of his youth had been
worn down, he had poured out his life, all that might
have been joy and beauty, discovery and revelation,
everything that life can be to a free soul—he had poured
it all into the ticker tape machines, and his story was
written in numerals instead of words . . . on a long thin
piece of paper tape.

Where was the wine of life and the soft voice of its
yearning? Where was the song of day and the silent
wonder of the night? Where were spring and summer?
The petals on the grass, the wings in the air? Where were
they? Where were friendship, love and beauty? All of
them snared and raveled, snarled and tangled, in the
twists and turns of yard after yard of long, thin paper
tape.

Mr. Kirby had not only failed to do what he wanted;
he had ceased to live as he wished. And that is the saddest part of all. It is possible to be defeated in what we
want to do, what we would choose as a vocation, and
still live in major part the life we want to live. It is possible, that is to say, if we recognize that life is not the
creature of circumstance. Indeed, in the whole universe
of everything that is, life alone, life by its very nature, is

the antagonist of circumstance. Inanimate things all drift. Water flows to the sea by the path of least resistance. But life climbs the mountains and conquers the wilderness and mounts into the sky. If there is any one thing that is utterly clear about the nature of life, it is that it was meant to master circumstance. At the human level, it is meant to master even its own circumstances—the oppositions within as well as the barriers without. The spirit conquers all things when the spirit wills it, and no excuse remains when we fail to live as we wish.

To live as we wish—again I stop for definition. I do not mean by *wish* the confused and fluctuating moods of lethargy or impulse. At this level, we have not yet reached the human quality of life. I mean the quality and intensity which only come through actual and deliberate choice, and by constantly renewed decision. Of this kind of life we must say that multitudes permit themselves only the passing hint of its existence.

We are afraid of our own wish for life: afraid of its joy with the penalty of equal sorrow, afraid of its beauty with the sting of transiency, afraid of its justice with the unremitting claim of the relentless, afraid of the soul—the soul that must lose the world to find itself and God.

Most of all, we are afraid of religion. So much so that we disguise it, tame it, put a halter on it. What was meant to be wings for the spirit we turn into a packhorse to carry the clay images of our own impostures, the faded finery of our worn and shoddy duperies. We do not listen to Jesus, telling us that he came, not to fetter lives but to make them more abundant. We do not recognize our likeness to the Scribes and Pharisees, rebuked by Jesus for their lifelessness, for not living zestfully and generously; for not living as their hearts moved them to live, for not living as they really wished. We want religion to protect and justify our pettiness; we change the wine of life for the brackish water of our turbid pieties.

To the lesser virtues, we say yes; to the bold adventure, no. The religion of audacious righteousness, of moral condemnation of entrenched evils, of vast obligation to a world sunken in misery and at the same time golden with opportunity—to this religion we say no. When we pray, we keep telling God how great *he* is, lest, if we paused for a moment, he should have a chance to call on *us* for greatness. And we keep him a long way off, lest he breathe into our nostrils the breath of his life and we become living souls.

It was this that caused Vachel Lindsay to cry out so bitterly at stifled imaginations and famine-shrivelled souls. We grow dull; we are ox-like, leaden-eyed, he said. That is the tragedy, "not that we die, but that we die like sheep." Surely he is right. Death was never such a tragedy as littleness of life. It is not so bad to die, but never to live the lives that we were born to live—that is the tragedy!

What is it that people do with their lives—lives that might have been large and generous, bold and adventurous, great in the scope of their thought, warm with imagination, audacious in some great act of faith, magnanimous in forgiveness, smilingly victorious over setbacks and disasters—what is it that happens to these lives? What do they ever gain that is half so precious as the opportunities they lose? How does it happen that so many lives, big in initial possibility, shrink and shrink until their days and nights are reckoned like the rise and fall of waves in an endless waste of ocean water?

Those lives we never live! That vision we almost fol-

lowed, wanted to follow! But we could have been defeated, we could have suffered, we could have been
humiliated; so we didn't follow. That word of truth we
might have spoken! But truth has a price—we might have
had to pay it. Embattled self-centeredness—we nearly
conquered it. Nobody but ourselves knows how near we
came to victory. Justice, too, was calling to us, and the
clean winds of righteousness were blowing through our
lives; we nearly gave up that prejudice, that malice, that
cherished resentment.

Something said, "You know the truth: face it!" We
nearly faced it. And again we heard the voice: "You
could be honest. You really could, you know. You could
change your opinion. You could say you were wrong and
were now ready to be right. You could surrender to the
only conqueror you can honorably submit to—your conscience." We *nearly* did it. Nearly lived the life we
wanted to live. Then we turned away. For we remembered that this isn't the way the world gets along. You
must do as the world does if you want to get along the
way the world gets along. And so we let the moment go.
The life that might have been departed and was lost in
the No-Man's-Land of the Lives We Almost Lived.

Until one day we sat down and wondered what we had
received in return for giving up what we really wanted
to be and do. We found ourselves looking at the years
that had brought us nothing—and at the years ahead with
nothing left to bring.

How pathetic it is that people can come so close to the
loveliness of life and never make room for it. Or can feel
the generous impulse of it and still suppress it. Though
again and again they *nearly* find this quality of life—and
nearly live it.

I remember, many years ago, in an overseas parish, trying to reconcile the parents of an only daughter to a marriage she was going to make with a man who was unacceptable in the social circles in which this family moved. He was a good man, and full of promise, and the two young people loved each other with a devotion that warmed my heart.

But the boy came from "the wrong side of the tracks," and the bride's parents would have nothing of him. I did my utmost to persuade them to attend the wedding. "No," said the mother, "I will not lend myself to it! I will have nothing to do with it!" I tried every persuasion I could devise. "Think!" I said. "This only daughter was once a baby in your arms, the only baby you ever held to your breast and called your own. You watched its first smile, its eyes big with wonder, and you wept for joy. You saw the little girl grow up, year by year; you watched the mystery of her life's unfolding, you saw the girl becoming the woman, young and lovely, waiting without yet knowing it for the man whose image would fill her heart. Now he has come to claim her. The hand of life which is the hand of God is joining them together. Some day, you will hear that she, too, has a baby, and your mind will go back swiftly over the shortness of the years. You will feel a great yearning to hold your daughter's baby in your arms, a yearning that will grip you and hold you and will not let you go. What will you do in that day when you have to remember that you would not attend your daughter's wedding?"

My pleas were all in vain. The wedding took place, rather pathetically, with just two witnesses. There were hardly any flowers. But I thought it might be a kindness to write to the girl's mother, describing the brighter side of it, and I did. The next day, the mother came to see me. I never saw a more pitiful person. She could scarcely speak for sobbing. "I don't know why I did it," she said. "I wanted to come. Inside of me, I wanted to come. I knew it was right. I nearly did come. But, oh God! oh God! I didn't."

Nearly! The things we *nearly* do! The lives we *almost* live! I have no doubt that Judas nearly decided not to betray Jesus. He loved Jesus. Everything that was decent in him pled with him to stand by and carry loyalty to the uttermost proof. He knew it at the time and suppressed the knowledge of it. But when he knew it again, he could suppress it no longer; for he was counting the thirty pieces of silver. So he went out and hanged himself.

I have no doubt the judges of Socrates nearly declared him innocent. Each one of them severally. For they all knew. But they were afraid of themselves and of each other. And so they went, each of them, to the end of his days, remembering the long slow smile of Socrates while he listened to the verdict.

Yet none of this need ever be so. We could live those lives we nearly live. In our moments of deliberate thought we know beyond all question that no alternative is worth considering. We know that in the few short years we spend here it is folly to do anything less. The call is strong within us—the call to live. To live from the fullness of the heart. To live as we might live.

II

Courage Is What You Do About It

IN JOHN BUNYAN'S *famous allegory,* Pilgrim's Progress, *it is related that Christian, as
he mounted Hill Difficulty, came upon two
men running down the hill to meet him. The
name of one was Timorous, and of the other,
Mistrust. To these two men he said,* "Sirs,
what's the matter? You run the wrong way."
*To which they replied that near the top of
the hill they had found* "a couple of lions in
the way, whether sleeping or waking we
know not, and we could not think, if we
came within reach, but that they would
presently pull us in pieces."

Then said Christian, "You make me afraid,
but whither shall I fly to be safe? I must
venture. To go back is nothing but death; to
go forward is fear of death . . . I will yet go
forward." *So Mistrust and Timorous ran
down the hill, and Christian went on his way.*

*When he approached the lions his fear
grew greater, but on coming closer he found
them chained. He thereupon went forward,
keeping to the middle of the road, and although the lions roared so that he shook and
trembled,* "they did him no harm."

8

Too Many People Stay Afraid

THERE IS NOTHING new about fear. It is as old as the first
living creature that could sense the approach of danger.
For millions of years, while life ascended from the lower
to the higher levels, fear was its protection. It warned the
physically weaker animals to keep away from enemies
that were stronger. It impelled them to take flight instead
of trusting in an ineffectual boldness, and thus preserved
them from extinction.

Nor was it otherwise when the human level was
reached. For man is one of the physically weaker animals.
If he had not been afraid of the tiger and the wolf, the
serpent and the alligator, he would never have learned to
defend himself against them. Fear was a spur, a goad.
Because of it, all manner of exertions were undertaken.
And these, in the end, made man the master of the earth,
afraid of nothing but his fellow-man.

I do not mean that this was done through fear; it is more
true to say that it was done through courage. But then,
what is courage but the conquest of fear? There is nothing courageous in doing something that you are not
afraid of; courage emerges because fear has called it forth.
Moreover, to be useful, courage must not be blind. Fear
must make it clear-sighted and alert. There must be a
realistic reckoning with the adversary. Otherwise, however splendid, no amount of courage will avail.

It is meaningless, therefore, to say as Thomas Carlyle

once did, that "we must get rid of fear." A living creature devoid of fear would be a freak, a biological monstrosity. It would lack the instinctive responses necessary for survival. If a human being were thus deprived, he would drown before he learned to swim, or crack his skull before he learned to walk, or be run over because he stood too long in the path of an onrushing automobile.

What sense does it make, then, to say that fear should be banished? It *cannot* be banished, and if it could be, the world would be a madhouse. Let us acknowledge, then, that fear has a place in life. Who would want to serve in an army commanded by a general so blindly daring as to risk his troops being massacred? Who would care to be operated upon by a surgeon who never feared that he might make a mistake? Fear means awareness: awareness of danger, awareness of limitations, awareness which impels restraint.

That is what it should always mean, whether in a personal life or an international situation. We should have no patience with those who tell us that there is nothing in the world crisis to be anxious about, that everything is sure to be all right, that all we need do is banish our fears. To take this attitude is really cowardice, and one of the most dangerous forms of cowardice. What is there that is brave about unwillingness to face the facts? Just as some people frighten themselves into helpless pessimism, so others intimidate themselves into foolish optimism. Fears are not things to turn your back upon any more than they are things to drown in. What we must do is face them—and that is what courage is—that to begin with. Courage is what we do with situations of which we are afraid.

Where would the courage of primitive man have been if he had refused to see that the jungle was full of enemies? How could he have survived if he had told himself that none of these enemies were really dangerous, that all he had to do was walk through the jungle unafraid? What he actually did was to recognize the perils by which he was surrounded, admit that they were frightening, and then work out ways of defeating them. His courage produced, not a shallow and fatal optimism but a patient search for weapons and a willingness for the hard work that built up barricades. Presently, it provided him, as we have already said, with complete mastery. Courage was not the absence of fear; *courage was what he did with fear.*

The same requirement still prevails. We shall not be helped in the least by the delusion that courage is how some people *feel* about danger, and how other people do not. Courage is how some people *deal* with danger, and after a while their way of dealing with it becomes a habit.

What a strange thing it is that in spite of living in an age of popular psychology, so many people resist one of the simplest insights that psychologists have tried to teach, namely, that to turn away from something or to hide it and repress it is the surest possible way of making it more troublesome. Instead of being ordinarily anxious, you then become neurotically anxious, obsessionally anxious; and instead of placing your fears where you can deal with them rationally and resolutely, you swallow them up in the inner darkness of your 'unconscious' where they have an unimpeded opportunity of sapping your courage secretly and of making you emotionally weak and depressed.

To master fears—I do not say to banish them but just to gain control over them—you must first of all face them. How can we deal effectually with disagreeable realities if we refuse to look at them and see what they are like? Until we have done this, there is no hope whatever of becoming less afraid.

Courage begins, then, with the facing of fear. And unfortunately, this is what a great many people refuse to do. Consequently, they are undermined by fear. Their situation is like that described by Coleridge in *The Ancient Mariner,* who speaks of

> . . . one, that on a lonesome road,
> Doth walk in fear and dread,
> And having once turned round, walks on,
> And turns no more his head,
> Because he knows a frightful fiend
> Doth close behind him tread.

But what must we do when we face our fears? Shall we stand and let ourselves be paralyzed? Or, rushing to the opposite extreme, shall we take a deep breath and invite ourselves to believe for no good reason at all that things are not as bad as they appear? We are foolish if we do either of these things. What we need to do is consider the situation as it actually is. Then we should reckon up what we have—or can come to have—with which to meet it. And it is here, of course, that we come to the parting of the ways.

If primitive man had decided that the strength of the lion and the stealth of the panther were too much for him, in that instant he would have been defeated. But because he noticed that he had something with which the other animals could not compete—intelligence—and because he was willing to use this gift to attain power and skill, he learned to hurl spears into lions and to lay traps

for panthers and in the end to put the animal realm beneath his feet.

What we decide to do when we face our fears is almost
entirely a matter of resolve. If we tell ourselves that our
resources are not enough, we tell ourselves the truth, for
by so saying we have *made* them not enough. This is the
case no matter what the situation, a nation's or an individual's. But if we look our fears steadily in the face and
decide that there is something we can do about our situation, that is the beginning of courage. If we can say to
ourselves, not too loudly but loudly enough for our own
hearts to hear it plainly, "I think I can do whatever has
to be done," once again we have very likely told ourselves the truth. The decision is our own. For courage is
not how we *feel*—at any rate, not at the beginning—but
what we *do* about it.

Nor do we ever help our situation by refusing to face
it, hoping that if we close our eyes we can expect the
difficulties somehow to disappear. Some day—the chances
are always in favor of it—we shall have to face what we
fear anyway. Then, in unavailing desperation we will
fight. But it may be too late. As Shakespeare puts it,

> Cowards fight when they can fly no further,
> As doves do peck the falcon's piercing talons.

It is a bitter metaphor: a dove, caught beyond the possibility of escape, uselessly pecking at the piercing claws
that hold it helpless in a vise-like grip!

By facing what we fear before it is too late and by
acting resolutely, we can avoid this fate. Again and again,
the individual, caught in a net of misfortune, refuses to
face the realities while he still has the power of dealing

with them. He is afraid of the exertions needed and of the likelihood of pain and loss. Yet, it is by acting *then,* as soon as the threatening circumstances challenge him, and not by waiting with his face averted until all hope is gone, that the individual can decide the issue. What he can do may at the first be very little. But little added to little becomes enough. In the end, he gains the mastery. But to do this he must face what he fears with open eyes, understanding that courage is not what he *feels* but what he *does* about it.

It is the same with a nation. If we had not been afraid to look at facts in the nineteen thirties—very disagreeable facts—there would have been no Second World War. We could have prevented it. Similarly, if we are to master our present threatening circumstances, we must know with utter clearness what our dangers are, and then, with quiet, deliberate resolution, act accordingly to wear these dangers down.

Never since the beginning of time has peace been built on fear. Peace can only be built on courage—the courage that is what we do with fear. Nor must we think of courage as requiring always immediate, harsh, audacious action. Courage is firmness, fortitude, determination. Courage calms the mind, not inflames it. Courage allows time for wise decisions. Courage can be patient as well as prompt. The highest form of courage is not audacity but fortitude.

There are many more pleasing words, I know, than this word *fortitude.* It carries a suggestion of something long drawn out, a hint of grimness. We prefer, no doubt, the showy sort of courage, bravery in the sense of something brief but daring. But the likelihood is—and to win we must face it—that fortitude is the kind of courage we shall chiefly need.

By fortitude, however, we do not mean something merely stolid and impassive. There is a world of difference between the aliveness of fortitude and the deadness of despair. To remember what we *do* mean, let us recollect a famous story.

Through the summer of 1787, a prolonged debate was wearing itself out in a well known hall in Philadelphia. Day after day, differences that seemed irreconcilable were receiving new emphasis as speaker answered speaker in heated and sometimes acrimonious argument. It had begun in the middle of May, and now it was Monday, the 9th of July. In the chair, "entertaining motions, putting questions, announcing votes," was the most respected man in America. His face was expressionless and no one could know how near he was to hopelessness. The colonies he had led to victory in a war for independence would fail, it seemed, to build security upon their victory. The union of the states would never be consolidated.

A friend of the chairman, a brilliant young statesman from New York, had given up the conference in disgust. The chairman was thinking about him, and of how this man had fled when his own plan for a union of the states was given no consideration.

And so George Washington took up his pen and commenced a letter to Alexander Hamilton. It was a candid letter: candid about Washington's own feeling, his own opinion of the proceedings; but candid, also, in its reproach to Hamilton. It was not offensive—Washington was never that. It was considerate, and yet the reproof was plain.

"I *almost* despair," he wrote, (he underlined the word 'almost') "of seeing favorable issue to (these) proceedings, and do therefore repent having had any agency in the business." Those who were obstructing agreements, he continued, were "narrow-minded politicians" and hypocritical concerning the real cause of their opposition. But, he concludes to Hamilton, "I am sorry you went away. I wish you were back. The crisis is equally important and alarming, and no opposition under such circumstances should discourage exertions till the signature is fixed."

The crisis is "equally important and alarming!" Was ever the obligation of a crisis more perfectly implied? The extent to which it is alarming is the measure of its urgency, the compulsion of its claim. If you are afraid of what might happen, you must increase your exertions. For courage is not the way you feel—you can feel sorry that you ever "had any agency in the business"—but courage is what you *do* about it. And when you *go on doing it,* irrespective of the fluctuations of despair and hope, that is the noblest kind of courage—*fortitude.*

And so you *do* go on. Not in a half-hearted, desperate sort of way, but vigorously, determinedly. You go on with all you've got. Until, like Washington, you can announce at last the consummation of your purpose. Or—for this, too, can happen—until you are yourself defeated but leave behind a task made easier for those who follow. Which also, though the world knows it not, is true success.

The future will be claimed, not a doubt of it, by those whose endurance is greatest. How far it is from here to there, no one can tell. Or all that must be met with in the way. But this we can know: from the beginning until now, victory has been the fruit of courage, the reward of fortitude. And it always will be.

9

Is There a Cure for Frustration?

LET US BEGIN on a lowly level. Frustration is found, the psychologists tell us, not only in human beings but in animals. Individuals of any species, if their resources are overtaxed, display similar symptoms. Rats, for instance, may be placed in a labyrinth and will try repeatedly to learn the right turnings, bringing them perhaps to a food supply located at the exit. If the food supply is left in the same place and the turnings of the labyrinth are not too frequently altered, the rats will make a satisfactory adjustment. If, however, the windings of the labyrinth are repeatedly changed, or the food is placed where it seems inaccessible, the rats will gradually lose confidence, and after a while in spite of hunger will give up the effort.

Other animals, overtaxed by similar complexities, will do the same. From species to species, the degree of resourcefulness will vary—as it also will with different individuals. But past a certain point the result will always be the same: the animal gives up and begins to die. Sometimes it is a quiet proceeding, as though hopelessness had caused a sort of paralysis. At other times, the animal will go through several phases: at first, panic, leading it to waste its energies; then spitefulness, provoking it to turn savagely on whatever living creatures are nearest to it—other members of its own species, most likely, companions in the same misfortune, maddened by the same distress. Then its energies begin to languish and apathy sets in. It

[87]

may be difficult at this point to revive it; it has begun to die.

This, then, in barest outline, is the pattern of frustration as observed by those who have undertaken animal experiments. In other cases, controlled conditions have not been necessary; some animals, no matter how easy life may be made for them, wither away just because they have been placed in captivity. Or their behavior changes; they become unpredictable. Thoroughly adjusted to a familiar set of conditions, they are completely helpless when faced with new ones. They are unable to put forth the effort required, or perhaps we should say unwilling. In any case, they soon exhibit symptoms of frustration.

All of which, of course, would be interesting only in a zoological sort of way if it had no application to human beings. We would like to say that at our own level, with reason to guide us, everything is quite different. The mind of man is a far more powerful instrument than the intelligence of animals. Man can perceive his circumstances and see into his problems more readily. For him, therefore, fortified by intellect, no frustration is necessary. He can make whatever adjustments are required.

We wish we could say this. Unfortunately, however, it does not always seem to happen so. To a quite startling extent, human behavior resembles that of animals. An individual man or woman, thrown out of a familiar environment, may show symptoms of frustration remarkably similar to those we have been describing. We might cite, for instance, the once-prosperous individuals who committed suicide in the depression of the 1930's. They were not starving, nor ever likely to starve. But they could not face what seemed to them adversity. In almost everything they really wanted to do, they felt frustrated. And thus, they allowed themselves to become depressed and life lost its interest.

I remember that in those years—I lived near New York City at the time—I was called upon occasionally to try to help people who were suffering from this condition. Sometimes it would be a man—a business man—who found himself unwilling or unable to tell his wife and children of their reduced circumstances; and he would mention to me that he had been thinking of suicide. Which, of course, was utter folly and would have meant a far heavier blow to his family than the loss of fortune or position. Yet, the frustrated individual can reach this point; he is resigned to die rather than brace himself for unfamiliar conditions. The path through the labyrinth seems closed to him; he has tried one turning after another and none of them leads to where he wants to go. It has not occurred to him —not yet—that he is free to jump out of the labyrinth, that is to say, free to adjust himself to new and different expectations.

We may also remember—and this was a far more grievous case—the wave of suicides in Austria just before the Hitler invasion. Defense was hopeless; to live under the Nazi regime was unspeakably degrading; what was there, then, to live for? Death was the only answer.

So it seemed to some—though not, of course, to the majority. There were those who lived to resist the Nazi conquest, to fight it by every means they found available, and in the end to win. Close as they were to despair, they went on resisting it.

We must admit, also, I am afraid, that human individuals can share with animals some of the other symptoms of frustration. Panic, for instance. Instead of guiding their energies into deliberate and rational activity, they waste them in frenzied behavior. Then comes the second stage, when panic induces helplessness and leaves them paralyzed. This sequence reminds us of the literal derivation of the word, *frustration*, namely, *in vain*. To be frustrated means to be reduced to futility, to find conditions too much for you, or yourself unequal to them, so that—if the impasse persists—you are incapable of useful effort and surrender to despair.

It is also true, I think, that human individuals, driven by frustration, will sometimes turn upon each other, just as animals are prone to do. Instead of cooperating, which would make them masters of their situation, they tear each other apart, which seals their doom. If rats in a labyrinth could organize their activities they could chart all the turnings, and every time one was changed could make the necessary adjustments. Conceivably they could make ladders of their own bodies, and if there were enough of them, climb right out of the labyrinth. Their helplessness is partly due to their inability to cooperate.

But how different is it with a human society? Orderly activity, well planned and courageously and patiently carried out, could often have saved a civilization which, for lack of it, was doomed to perish. None of the symptoms of frustration is more frightening than this tendency of the sorely beset to vent their rage upon each other precisely at the moment when salvation depends upon the will to cooperate.

And all of this, let us notice, can be understood by treating the question merely at the level of experimental psychology. I have not drawn at all as yet upon the higher wisdom, or quoted the prophets and the sages, or appealed to the teachers of religion. We can get a grasp of the matter—the essentials of it—without believing anything that recent observation does not verify.

A human society, subjected to rapid and drastic changes, is just as likely as any other form of life to feel itself unequal to the altered circumstances. We used to speak of this as the difficulty of getting people to adjust their horse-and-buggy thinking to the age of the automobile. But long before this had been accomplished, the automobile was an obsolete symbol and we were asked to adjust to the age of aviation. Admonishing ourselves to feel exhilarated, we were doing the best we could to get our thinking off the ground when we were suddenly informed that everything whatever had been superseded: a new dimension had entered human life and unless we proved equal to it, atomic energy would blow us off the planet.

Nor was this all. Having fought one war to put an end to the old-fashioned kind of aggression and another to expel a new and worse variety, we were now faced with the most menacing aggression of all. Some of our allies in the First World War were our enemies in the Second, and our enemies in the Second we hoped to make our allies in the Third—if there had to be a Third. And exactly where we stood it was difficult to know.

We did not want this kind of world. We did not want a split atom. We did not want enemies. We did not want allies. We did not care who was "peace-loving" and who wasn't. We wished we could get back to a world that we could understand and cope with. We would even take sides with the peace-loving horse-and-buggy against the fire-breathing automobile!

And so we came to feel frustrated. Not that these rapid words have painted the complete picture. There was a good deal else—new kinds of knowledge, new beliefs and disbeliefs, new things that happened to the family, new stridencies in human relationships, and of course, much more. I do not need to describe it all. It is the world we live in. The world, also, of new hopes which have made ancient evils intolerable: new hopes of justice, of security, of prosperity, of peace. And the world of resistance to these hopes. It is a complicated picture—who can portray it? But it is also the world we live in—and the world that frustrates us.

Can anything be done about it? Can frustration be cured? There are those, apparently, who think the answer to be no; they feel that it cannot be cured. They do not say so openly, but their whole attitude, as well as the implications of what they do say, is that the situation is too much for us and that sooner or later we must expect defeat. I do not share this attitude. I do not even admire those who are preparing to go down bravely, singing the *liebestod* of a dying culture before they are engulfed. I believe that we can win—in the world situation and in our personal lives alike—and that we need not be frustrated. Whether we *do* win depends not upon an implacable fate but upon the quality of our own resolve.

To cure frustration, four things, I think, are necessary: *first, a clear aim.* We must know what we intend to do. Every factor in our situation should be thoroughly evaluated. Then we should decide upon the best procedure. Frustration will begin to diminish as soon as we know what we mean to do. We need, for instance, in our present international situation, a clearly defined purpose—what might be called a spelled-out aim. With such an aim we can invade every country in the world—not militarily but spiritually—and no iron curtain can keep us out. No one is frustrated when he is going somewhere, no matter how difficult the journey; frustration is when you are going around in circles, or standing still.

Second, we need a *patient courage.* Panic, which as we have seen, is one of the symptoms of frustration, comes from desperation, the unseating of reason, the feverish but useless response to something that frightens us. We need courage—yes, but a special kind of courage: *patient courage.* Courage that thinks, decides, and moves deliberately towards a chosen end. Not sporadic courage or the valor of despair—but hardihood, endurance, fortitude.

There are no problems of the modern world that are truly insoluble. Every question that the present crisis poses can be answered—every last one. There is not a task before us that cannot be accomplished. The intelligence that was equal to discovering the secret of the atom is equal to these other challenges. But success will come—if we decide to succeed—not through intelligence that is merely potential but through the intelligence that we diligently use, and through the untiring and enduring courage that leaves nothing to chance, that takes up every part of our situation and deals with it patiently and tenaciously. If we can once get ourselves into the frame of mind where courage of this sort is invited, frustration will fall away.

The *third* thing is *cooperation.* I have already implied the importance of this by pointing out that even the experimental animals used by the psychologists could solve their problems through cooperation, if they were capable of it. Human societies are governed by the same requirement. It was Jesus who told us how hopeless is the situation of a house divided against itself, and Lincoln used this metaphor in a speech that roused the nation.

It is a saying with many applications. In a family situation where difficult conditions have to be met, such as impoverishment or removal to an unwelcome location, the family, instead of blaming one another and thus depleting the hopefulness and energy of each of its members, must cooperate, thereby steadily overcoming the handicaps while building up powers of endurance.

A nation, when facing an emergency, must unite the energies, the loyalties, the zeal, the power to act, of all its citizens in a disciplined and resolute endeavor. When its people cease fighting one another—spiteful and embittered because the world is not the pleasant world they wanted—and concentrate upon their enemies whose evil aims are threatening general ruin and dissolution, they break the fetters of frustration.

I am not supposing that cooperation is easy. Nor do I mean by it a regimented point of view, numbed by conformity. What I do mean can easily be illustrated. If a number of people are rowing a life-boat through a storm and some of them think safety lies in following one course and others another, they must come to a decision. The minority may dissent from this decision—that is to say, they may think that it is not the best decision. But nevertheless, when it comes to rowing they must bend their backs to the oar and pull just as hard as the majority. If, from time to time, the crew stops to rest for a minute, the minority is entitled to speak up and say why the course should be changed. If a point can be carried, they should carry it. But nevertheless, when the boat moves on, every man's heart must be in his rowing. That is what I mean by cooperation.

The *fourth* necessity is *faith*. This might be stated as a strong conviction that what is right deserves to triumph and that if we serve it faithfully we have a chance to win. There will be those who, having said that much, would leave it at that. I think, however, that for those who seek it and test it in experience, those who are willing to be patient and not expect too much at first, there comes to be a deeper faith: faith in the moral law that works in history, faith in justice as rooted in the law that rules the universe, faith in the ultimate upon which all things else must rest—faith in God.

After all, if the world had *not* frustrated us, how do we know that it would have been better for us? Suppose all our utopias, public and private, had somehow come true, would the greatness of life have been more or less? There was once a preacher, a friend of mine tells me, who went to heaven and was bitterly disappointed. Heaven, he discovered, was exactly as he had described it to his congregation! Suppose our heavens-on-earth had all materialized? The world and everything within it might well have been unbearable.

It was not a very good world, you know, this world that is so swiftly changing. That is why countless millions are in revolt against it. They never shared its benefits. Such a world was sure to change. How could it endure?

Faith in God means that when the dark days are over, there will be a better world. We may not live to see it; no, but we shall not be frustrated if we live to make it possible, if we give it our utmost, convinced that it is on its way. Faith in God—a reasonable, honest, true belief, not an escapism—means that frustration will lose its power over us. For in its presence, we no longer ask as much for ourselves as we did. We belong to something larger, something greater than our own purposes. Like Washington, who pledged his "life, his fortune, and his sacred honor" to the best he knew, we can say at last with minds at rest, "the event is in the hands of God."

10

Can Anxiety Be Mastered?

THERE IS ONE thing, at least, which anxious people will find plentiful, namely, advice. But the more they consider this advice, the more they will discover that the difficulty is not in giving it but in taking it.

"Anxiety does no good," says the psychologist; "it lowers efficiency, dissipates energy, lessens the emotional force you need with which to face your problems. Therefore, get rid of it." "Yes, indeed," the anxious person replies, "there is nothing in the world I am more desirous to do; but how?" And at that point, unfortunately, the adviser seems to lose his fluency. "What is the use," you say, "of being told to stop being anxious, if you are not told how?" For if you had known how, you would not have needed to seek advice in the first place.

It reminds one of the patient whose doctor told him that what he needed was a trip around the world. "Doctor," the patient replied, "not only can I not afford a trip around the world, but I am wondering whether I can afford your fee for telling me to take one!"

Which, in turn, is no worse than the case of the minister who suggested curing anxiety by prayer. "Didn't that do some good?" he asked, after praying with the anxious parishioner. "It may have done God some good," the parishioner replied, "but me—I feel just about the same."

It is not only the modern psychologists, however, who command us to stop being anxious; the ancient sages and

the prophets of religion give the same advice. It is sooth-
ing, sometimes, to listen to the words in which they give
it. "Be not anxious for your life; consider the lilies of the
field, how they grow; they toil not, neither do they spin";
or "The Lord is my shepherd, I shall not want. He leadeth
me beside the still waters. He restoreth my soul." Such
words as these are beautiful and consoling just in the very
sound of them. And there are other such passages in
the ancient philosophers, such as Marcus Aurelius or
Epictetus.

But still, if we are entirely candid, we have to admit
that the effect of listening to these words wears off. Perhaps it shouldn't, but it does. We do not quite know what
is transmitted by such words, or what resources they are
intended to invoke. Perhaps what they mean is that we
could all, if we wished, live a much simpler life. Possibly
an entirely simple life, like that, for example, of St. Francis of Assisi. It is true, apparently, that St. Francis *did* live
a simple life, and made a notable success of it.

Yet, it has to be admitted that most of us are *not* like
St. Francis—not like him in the least; and furthermore,
that in the modern world, this may in some respects be
rather fortunate. Let us be honest. If everyone began
behaving exactly as St. Francis did, say at 8 a.m. tomorrow, the result would be disastrous. For the modern world
is the modern world and it is of no use pretending that it is
something simpler.

The experiment in simple living *has* been tried, of
course, in recent times, by the Mahatma Gandhi. He lived
simply, wove his own cloth, ate frugally . . . we know the
story. But he needed the telegraph and the newspaper, or
how would his influence have been spread abroad? He may
not always have *read* the news, but he certainly intended

to *make* the news—and did it very successfully. Although
his personal life was greatly simplified, he was nevertheless a part of a complicated, mechanized modern world,
and remained this no matter what he did, and being a
saint of considerable talent and perspicuity, he knew it.
After all, Gandhi was once a lawyer and a brilliant one,
and therefore, he never forgot the jury—which, in his case,
was the world, and he had to use modern methods for the
world to hear him.

And—I say this with deep respect—the modern world
remains a very complicated world, which could not possibly be run by nothing but Gandhis. Probably he himself
would have agreed to this. Not many saints really expect
to see themselves mass-produced.

No, we have to take the modern world pretty much as
it is, complexity and all. And we have to try to *solve* its
problems—not abandon them. The literally simple life is
not available.

Very well, then, what *is* available? Can anxiety be
mastered? I think the answer depends in the first place
upon what we mean by "mastered." If we mean banished,
then I think that for most people it is expecting too much.
Not that anxiety could *not* be completely done away with
by the perfect application of the principles applying to it.
The difficulty lies in achieving such a perfect application.
Anyone who had liberated within himself the resources
with which to do it would be so perfect in the first place
that he would never have found anxiety a problem.

No, when we say "mastered" I think we should be candid. I think we should define our expectation and the area
of application. We must leave out, for example, patho-
logical forms of anxiety, such as anxiety neuroses. I know
that normalcy shades off gradually into these abnormal

states, but we have to imagine a line of demarcation somewhere. We must also forsake the hope of ever reaching
perfect equanimity—on any basis. Most of us have to
admit that our moods will change; and so will the circumstances to which they respond. We will be anxious sometimes, no matter what we do about it. We may not always
have health enough, the physical support for mental calm.
We can get very tired and overwrought. We can lose the
wholesomeness that goes with health. When this takes
place, we will be likely to be anxious.

In what sense, then, can we use the word "mastered"?
In the sense, I think, that we can speak of mastery of
anything human—that is to say, it will be fallible and
incomplete and liable to interruption. Just as we say that
we have mastered the air and yet we have aeronautical
accidents, or that we have mastered certain diseases and
yet people die because we cannot always cure them. All
human mastery is incomplete. In this limited sense—a
reasonable sense, and, I believe, a true one—we *can* relieve
and master our anxieties. We can keep them under control;
we can prevent them, for the most part, from using up
too much of our energy, or greatly lowering our efficiency
or dissipating our morale. How?

Let me try to give the answer, so far as I know it, in
terms that are utterly practical. There are four principles
or rules, which, taken together, will give us mastery over
anxiety, at least a great deal of the time.

The first is: *Face the realities.* Nothing is so terrible
when you face it as when you run away from it. Now, the
first reality, and one which superficial sorts of religion try
to mask or hide, is that of *limited security.* We live on a
spinning ball, all but the outer crust of which is flame; we
live on it subject to all its hazards and we always will:

these include earthquake and hurricane, tornado and erup-
tion, storm and avalanche, fire and flood. We live our
physical lives within our own precarious bodies, subject
to all the perils of disease, all the dangers of accident. We
live our mental lives subject to all the chances of error, all
the possibilities that reason itself may be unseated. Anything we have may at any time be taken away. When we
rebel against misfortune and are bitter because of loss,
we have forgotten that life has never given us any guar-
antees. In spite of all the title-deeds that fill the vaults of
banks, not one of us securely owns a single thing. For a
few short years with all their hazards, we have the use of
them and that is all. There is nothing that we call our own
which may not at any time be lost.

Yes, and in spite of all that we may do for our own
security, and in spite of all that human society may add
to this to make us safer—and I think human society should
do its best—nevertheless, safety and security will always
be flimsy things, easily blown away. That is why the sages
and the prophets are absolutely practical when they tell
us not to depend upon material things. It is not just a
question of whether it is right or wrong to do so; it is
a question of whether it is intelligent. The plain fact is
that material things are not dependable. It is therefore
folly to depend upon them. To do so is to build a house
upon sand. When the storm comes, it is likely to be washed
away. The first reality, therefore, is the reality of limited
security. We should all make friends with it, because it
will be with us all our lives.

We must also face the realities in other ways. We must
face the realities about ourselves. We must try to estimate
our own capacities and abilities with candor. We must
know our own deficiencies. We must bring everything to

the surface and keep it there for long enough to absorb it and base our judgments upon it. Just as many people never make their peace with the insecurity of the world they live in, so others never make their peace with their own real selves—what, nowadays, they call their personalities. Just what is any one of us entitled to in this world? Just what do we deserve? Just what can we truly attain? How should we rate our claim?

I say with the utmost emphasis that the sooner each one of us understands that nothing is *owed* to him, that all he has is just a gift that he cannot possibly establish a right to, the sooner will he find his soul at peace. Today there may be the blue sky and the green earth and the eyes that see them; today there is health and strength; today there are friends and loved ones; today there is a little happiness; let us take them today, for tomorrow we do not know. The present moment is the only moment we can live in. The past comes with us, it is true; and the future is before us and we must aim our lives towards it; but they both meet in the swiftly moving present and they can never meet anywhere else. Let us accept this as a basic reality, for that is what it is. It does not mean living without memory. It does not mean ceasing to face the future constructively. Far from it. But it does mean that all the satisfactions of any sort that we have *for ourselves* are in the present and that the present as it exists at any given moment cannot be perpetuated.

Of course, there is another side to this. The real is not merely rigorous and precarious. It is also often better than we think. Imagination is sometimes morbid. People allow themselves to be beset by fears that better understanding would soon prove slenderer or even groundless. Everyone

knows, I suppose, the little verse of rhymed wisdom which
runs as follows:

> As I was going up the stair,
> I met a man who wasn't there;
> He wasn't there again today—
> O how I wish he'd go away!

A great many fears—anxious fears—fall into that category. They are based upon such things as other people's
opinions (often people whose opinions don't count, anyway), on hypochondriac obsessions with imaginary illness,
on a feeling of persecution, or neglect, on a far-off threat
of poverty—on a hundred things of an infinitely varied
sort, none of which are especially likely to be actual.

Discover the realities, then! *Face* the realities! You
cannot live your life of ten years hence today. You cannot
live your life of one year hence today. You cannot live
your life of tomorrow today. But you can live today. And
you will be happier if, for whatever belongs to yourself,
you live with modest expectations, for whatever comes to
you that exceeds them is that much extra happiness. You
have no claim—remember it always!—everything that
comes to you comes of grace and bounty. Accept it joy-
fully but don't clutch it too tightly. Face the realities.
Develop a clear recognition of life's natural adventurous-
ness and make the most of it.

The second principle is: *Be energetic about the possibilities: and* ONLY *about the possibilities.* Altogether too
much energy and effort is expended upon *im*possibilities.
Thus anxiety is intensified by frustration. Many a man has
wasted his life trying to make it more secure than it can
possibly be made. Many a woman has wasted *her* life

trying to make her family safer than any family can possibly become. Remember that other people deserve to take some risks. Remember that you cannot get rid of risks yourself.

Concentrate upon what is possible. Try to find out exactly what it is—not too much in haste, certainly not in panic, but deliberately and steadily—and then, when you know, work at it. You may not be able to go precisely where you originally wanted to go; the world may not be the kind of world you used to think it was; much that is dear to you in it may not be available to your protection; but still, you can go *somewhere* and with credit and satisfaction; and the world may turn out to be doing better than you thought. As for what is dear to you, it may survive without your protection; and if not, you will find the courage that millions of others have found. Fit yourself into the actual opportunities: those you truly have or can really make. If you fail to do so by seeking the impossible, you will lose everything—including your joy in life.

We can truly say that running after the impossible brings on anxiety states more swiftly and more terribly than anything else. It can cause actual neurosis. It can produce embitterment. It is not true that we can have everything, do anything, achieve whatever we want to, though it *is* true that in the quality of our satisfactions we can live the lives that at our best we really want to live. Live, then, with the possible; cultivate the possible; find happiness in it and development and fulfillment. Do not succumb to the anxiety—the preventable anxiety—that disables us unnecessarily and paralyzes useful effort.

The third principle is: *Accept the inevitabilities.* What nothing can be done about should be accepted promptly and freely. We must not wait until it thrusts itself upon us as a crushing blow. Not many inevitabilities are intolerable. What *is* intolerable is anxiety about inevitabilities which are not accepted as such. I need hardly say that I am not advising inertia. I am not thinking of an indolent person's "inevitabilities" at all. I am thinking of such inevitabilities as the world of peril that we live in, and the world of change which hurries itself upon us.

I am thinking also of inevitabilities in the more narrowly personal life. "No man," said Jesus, "by being anxious can add one inch to his stature." If it cannot be done, do not fret yourself into a nervous breakdown trying to do it. And of course, Jesus was not concerned with mere physical height; he had in mind everything that cannot be changed no matter what we do about it—things that have to be accepted. And in the present world, there are many of them. To the inevitable it is best to bow—and, in its presence, to come at last to smile.

I think those are three pretty good rules—and quite practical. The more I have had recourse to them in my own life, the more I have come to see their worth. Face the realities; be energetic about the possibilities—and *only* the possibilities; accept the inevitabilities, freely, promptly and courageously. This may not banish anxiety—no—but it *will* cut down its power to thwart us and impede us; it *will* stop anxiety from eating into our hearts. It will give us some relief, something of mastery. And we can do these things—measurably—simply by trying; by beginning to do them and then going on doing them. Gradually, they become part of our life and we look out on the world with new recognition and insight.

I sometimes think I can identify the people who have this outlook—have it in a robust way—almost on sight. They do not have a hunted look. They have a special sort of laugh—or at least a smile. You know instinctively that in an emergency they would have strength. The strength that comes from wisdom and courage intermingled. It is very hard to put them out of countenance. They are almost free from pretense. If they do any pretending at all, it is for your sake, not their own. Within themselves, they are frank. They have met reality on its own terms. They are at peace with the truth of things. When they have to let go, they do so rather simply. When they hold on, they do it patiently and confidently.

Perhaps it is just this, after all, when carried far enough, that makes a sage or a saint. It is a total personal quality —and it comes with the mastering of anxiety. Of course, a great deal more could be said about it than this, but this is enough for the moment. It is the path to that deeper, truer kind of mastery: the mastery that looks at all the flashy sorts of achievement with a half-merry, half-pitying smile. Yet, it keeps a wary eye for pitfalls, knowing that no understanding and no mastery can ever be complete.

These three rules, then—*these and a fourth*. For though these rules are good, as I believe, I would not want to offer them alone. There is a *fourth*. *To master anxiety, or anything else whatever, a man must live for something bigger than himself*. Anxiety mainly comes from "I—me—mine." If we ourselves are all that life can hold of worth —all that is precious to us—then we are doomed before we start. We must get farther away from self-centered living. Live for other people—yes, and for the difficult but essential aims of the better world that we are trying to build. Just as the great artist becomes less absorbed in himself and more in his art, and as the true scientist devotes himself less to his fame and more to his quest, so must all men give themselves to what is more than they are—to the uttermost beyond them and the power of life within them, to the spirit of the highest and of God.

That is what we must do if we are ever to move in from the outer court of life's temple to its inner sanctuary. And when we do we can subordinate most other things, for everything falls into its own place. We do not clutch at life so fiercely when we feel that greater life has got its grip on *us*. For we belong, then, to the ultimate, to the invincible. We do not try to take it with us *our* way; we are ready to go with it, *its* way.

I said a while ago that all was insecure, that nothing was dependable. In the context that I spoke from then, what I said was true. But I speak now from a different context. I have raised the sights a little. And in the final sense, the sense which the soul knows by its own insight and experience, a great deal is dependable—indeed, everything that matters. Here is something that we cannot convey to each other by talking about it. It comes from living—patient, indomitable living.

When we come to know at last what it was that ancient men felt in their hearts when they cried out, "Into thy hands, O God," we know why all anxiety is needless. And between the mystery beyond us and the mystery within us, there is peace.

11

Personal Relationships in a Time of Crisis

ACCORDING TO VOLTAIRE, the most brilliant and mordant of satirists, the only thing left to do in a disordered world is to forsake it and dig in your own garden. At least, this is the opinion he puts into the mouth of Candide, the most famous of his characters. There are those, no doubt, who agree with it and would call it sound advice. This, however, is a matter scarcely worth arguing, since whether sound or otherwise, it is advice that cannot be taken.

Voltaire himself was unable to take it. This was partly because he was Voltaire but it was also because he was anybody. Human beings cannot live their lives as though there were nothing of life beyond themselves that they need be troubled with. If they confine themselves to their gardens, the world will invade their gardens. The problems they took no part in trying to solve will wash their barricades away and presently engulf them. There are no ivory towers, no havens of retreat, no islands of refuge where the modern individual will be left alone; wherever he goes the issues of the age will overtake him.

We are all involved—and cannot escape it—in a world of perils and upheavals. If we stop reading the newspapers, disconnect the radio and the television, ban public affairs from our conversation, we still cannot outlaw the questions that keep hammering at our minds, for these questions closely and persistently affect us. If we try to drive them out of sight, they become, so to speak, subversive activities; in the hidden places of our minds to which we have condemned them they lurk in the shadows, worrying us with vague forebodings, disquieting us with shapeless apprehensions, and it would be better if we brought them out into the light and took a look at them.

The fact is, and there is no denying it, that the winds of the world are blowing harshly upon us. Our personal lives are all encroached upon. Stridency is everywhere and day by day we suffer its intrusions. Thus we become fretted and easily exasperated, our tempers are chafed and touchy, we are irritable, soon angered, unreasonably ruffled and provoked. In a time of crisis, all relationships, even the most intimate and formerly dependable, are subject to strain. The stresses of the outer world are reflected in the inner world, and insecurity brings discord into the lives of families and friends.

Just as when we are sick we find it hard to bear annoyances which when we are well we hardly notice, so, when we are troubled in mind because of untoward events in the world outside, we become unduly sensitive and overly demanding in our personal relationships. If it goes far enough, we freeze our natural affections and become indifferent to those who love us; we are rough and inconsiderate, spoiling the happiness of others and greatly decreasing our own.

It is true, of course, that trouble makes some people kinder; with most, however, it is just the opposite. They would *like* to be kinder: at least, they think so in their moments of reflection; but the harshness of the world has entered into them and they are "edgy"; whatever they do, they do it with "raw nerves."

Worse than all this, there can be a real deterioration in our loyalties, an embittering of friendships and a decline in family morale. All sorts of doubts creep in. Is anything whatever worth it? The world outside seems to be pulling apart; can the inner world be held together? In the outer world, it seems to be everyone for himself; is it really any different in the home?

It is a strange and wistful thing that people are so prone to visit their resentments upon those they love. Often, they do it just because love seems to give them that privilege: they rely upon their loved ones, for love's sake, to bear it. But it is here, surely, that we need to stop and give ourselves a chance to think the matter through. The sympathy we need ourselves is one that other people need as well. By not inviting it we are wearing down our own resources and those of everybody else. What sense does it make?

Moreover, petulance is childish. The spoiling of other people's happiness is downright churlish. Is there anything that we are being peevish about that we might not—with a little effort, just a little honest effort—turn into drollery and laughter? Laughter is a much better emotional relief than petulance! Have we not sometimes seen a child in a stormy mood drawn gently by a tactful parent from the angry to the comic? Beginning with a tantrum he ends up with a chuckle. We might try this remedy ourselves.

Laughter is one of the most precious things in the world; in all creation, only man possesses it. But it is also one of the most useful things and can be cultivated. When people laugh together, it does not mean that they are taking things too lightly; those who laugh well are seldom frivolous. What it does mean is that they have found the secret of being serious without being somber, and of dissolving emotional strains with the aid of sympathy and kindness. I am speaking, of course, not of derisive laughter or the snickerings of scorn, but of the grin of candid self-appraisal, the smile of comprehension, the gentle and infectious comicality that smooths away an irritation, the laughter that can heal a hurt.

If our personal relationships are not to be damaged by the stresses of the time we live in, we must *cultivate* sympathy, not merely wish for it, and we must *practice* kindness, not wait for a genial mood to come upon us. Tenderness, clemency, gentleness, forbearance—these must be *invited*, and when they arrive, must be dissuaded from a transient visit and prevailed upon to stay. It is the same with the solace of laughter. When we feel the mood of irritation coming on, we should go before a mirror. We should say to the face we see in the glass, "Going to throw your weight about, hey? Going to snap at people? Going to cover everything with gloom? What a comic sort of character you are! Laugh at yourself, clown! No, not that kind of laugh! Try again! That's better. Now, go away and be decent to people. Happiness is precious. Find a little, share a little, make a little! Be as grown-up as you can."

Having said this much, however, all of it valid if we are willing to apply it, we must recognize some other factors. Especially in a time of crisis, there will be differences of opinion, and more than at other times such differences will be important. What can we do, then, with oppositions of viewpoint, within families and between friends? The members of a family may not always agree on vital issues; friends and intimates may be on opposite sides.

First, I think, we have to understand that separate persons are always separate persons, distinctive individuals with minds that can meet with other minds but cannot be absorbed or merged. Nothing is achieved by the attempt to dominate. Browbeating can never cure dissensions. What must be sought is patient, reasonable attitudes, honesty and fairness in discussion, and, if necessary—and quite often it may be necessary—agreement to differ. Even a married couple is composed of two people with two minds and two wills, and in spite of the words in the marriage service these two will not in all respects be one. But if they will be patient and really try to understand each other, both will benefit, even from a difference in opinion.

It is true that the happiest situation is when a family is like-minded. But where this is not the case, it is nothing but folly for a family to go "totalitarian." There is always a tendency for aggressive personalities to want to rule the views of other people. But this would be "thought control" transferred from the nation to the family. We should always remember that what goes on in the world at large is very similar to what goes on within our personal circles. The same motivations, the same frustrations, the same impatience, apply in the one case as in the other. If the problems of the outer world are to be resolved on the side of freedom, freedom must prevail in the inner world. It is the same with tolerance and goodwill.

The truth is that there is hardly any situation in which the soul is unable to grow. And the grown-up souls that are needed in the outer world will have to be developed in the inner world. If we realize this and are willing to act upon it, the whole question we are now discussing takes on a different and much more promising aspect. For instead of allowing the outer world to invade our personal lives, we can make our personal lives invade the outer world!

This is what the Apostle, Paul, would have called "the more excellent way." It consists of taking the spiritual offensive. Our personal problems, once mastered, make us wiser and stronger in dealing with all other problems. Our reinforcement of moral energy comes from the inwardness of our lives. If we can attain to this, the flame that burns on our hearthstones can be carried with us everywhere we go, lighting the way before us and warming the desolation of the world.

12

How Much Does the Individual Count?

I received a letter, not long since, from a man who thought he knew what should be done about some of the evils with which we are afflicted. "But," he said, "I myself am powerless to begin these things; I am unknown; I have no reputation; I am just an ordinary individual."

His attitude, I am afraid, is rather typical. People have come to believe that, except in small and insignificant ways, what they think and do is unimportant. They may have opinions but there is no way to give them weight; they may believe in a course of action but they feel helpless to initiate it. Decisions of consequence are all made by leaders—the very few who are vested with authority—and these few are not attentive to the opinions of ordinary people; they are affected only by mass opinion, and mass opinion can be manipulated.

If it happens, therefore, that something is being done that is clearly wrong, it is useless being incensed about it; what can you do? Wrongs can only be set right by legislative committees or crusading newspapers or through the personal tour-de-force of someone with commanding influence.

Suppose the government of your city is corrupt, its agencies of law enforcement undermined by bribery and graft—well, what can you do, except groan about it, and commiserate with your neighbor when you talk to him across the fence? You certainly can't fight your city gov-

[113]

ernment, and least of all its agencies of law enforcement. You would get nowhere—unless it were into trouble. Who are *you?* Nobody at all, just an ordinary individual.

Suppose you think that the behavior of some of those who have been elected to high places is foolish or hysterical, or even perhaps mean and sordid, well, you can tell your wife about it or the men who ride with you in your car pool, but what can you *do* about it? Except endure it, hoping that something will happen somewhere, sometime, that will change it? You are just one of the many, the vast multitude doomed to be helpless and inarticulate.

It may be that your school system is being attacked, that organized perfidy is secretly conspiring to destroy the reputation of your teachers, degrade your educational standards, shatter the confidence of the people in administrators who deserve to be trusted. This has happened in several American cities in the last few years. Well, what do you do? If you take a stand, will there be others to join you? Or will everyone be afraid—as you are—of having their loyalty impugned, of being called a traitor or a fellow traveler on the testimony of someone who saw you glance at a copy of the *Daily Worker* that had been left on the seat beside you on the train?

You are only an individual, an ordinary person with no influence, an anonymous member of a voiceless, faceless multitude, someone who doesn't count.

This, apparently, is the prevailing feeling. And if it persists, the Marxists will have scored a victory. What else is it but Marxist: the intimidation, the subjection, the complete subordination of the individual? To the extent, therefore, that we have this state of things in America, we are sick with the same disease that has cursed the peoples of the iron curtain countries. The virulence is less but the malady the same. We have come a little closer to being ants in an ant-hill.

Democracy as contrasted with Marxism is founded upon the significance of the individual. It is this significance that is fundamental and not the collective significance of the society. A democratic nation is not a field of grass, or a flock of sheep, or a colony of yeast cells; it is an association of free men and women. That was what was intended by the words, "life, liberty and the pursuit of happiness." Not totalitarian life, or collective liberty, or the pursuit of promulgated happiness; but individual life, individual liberty, and individual happiness. This does not mean, of course, that the individual exists apart from society, or that his life and liberty are unconnected with social relationships, or that all alone he can achieve his happiness. What it does mean is that the society shall liberate the individual and not dominate him; that it shall enhance his significance and not belittle him; that it shall respect him and not demean him. The government is his servant, not his master; his leaders are his agents, not his rulers; his fellow men are individuals like himself, his neighbors and his fellow citizens, not his fellow subjects. For democracy is founded upon the significance of the individual.

If this significance diminishes, if the individual feels weak and helpless, if he is afraid, intimidated, enfeebled by the palsy of futility, his society is to that extent Marxist rather than democratic, and has become infected with the virus of its enemies.

This is something to be thoughtfully considered. It was John Stuart Mill, one of the greatest exponents of individual significance, who warned us in his *Essay on Liberty* that "a state which dwarfs its men in order that they may be more docile instruments in its hands—even for benefi-

cial purposes—will find that with small men no great thing
can easily be accomplished."

The state that dwarfs its men deliberately and claims to
do so for beneficial purposes is, of course, the communist
state. But it is possible for people to become dwarfed without deliberate intention, without its being part of a plan.
We become dwarfed when we suffer the state of things
that is now obtaining in our own country. Listen again to
John Stuart Mill: "Whatever crushes individuality is des-
potism, by whatever name it may be called." Yes, despo-
tism because despotic in drift and inclination, despotic in
spirit and temper, despotic in tendency.

Ah, but you say, how can you be an individual in a
world of parties and factions? You have to go along with
what exists and choose from what there is, accepting its
limitations and endorsing the evil with the good. I wonder
if you do? Must a man be gagged by a lesser loyalty when
his conscience commands him to speak out for a higher
one? According to Thomas Jefferson, such a restriction is
beneath contempt. He never submitted his opinions, he
says, "to the creed of any party of men whatever, in religion, in philosophy, in politics, or in anything else. Such
an addiction is the last degradation of a free and moral
agent."

According to Jefferson, the individual may have a place
in a party and not be subject to the party. He can work
with other individuals in an organized movement and not
be restrained by the limitations of the group. Is this correct? Or must we modify it? Well, I will say this: it is not
certain that Jefferson, writing in his own time and out of
his own exceptional experience, entirely understood how
difficult this sort of independence might become. It is not
candid, I think, to pretend that an individual can work

with a group and not be disciplined by group procedures. Indeed, we should go further and admit that sometimes the individual will be submerged, temporarily, and his chosen purposes distorted if he works with a party or a movement.

But I think Jefferson would have replied to this that it is a matter of proportion; that beyond a certain point, the individual should rebel. His controlling loyalty should be to his convictions, and he should not get his loyalties confused. It is inconceivable to me that Jefferson would not exhort us, if he lived today, to reassert ourselves in character and conscience, as individuals. Only so can any of our associations—parties, movements, citizen groups, churches, or anything else—be carried to a higher level. There is no such thing as a society apart from the individuals who compose it. We speak of churches doing things, or of the Senate doing something, or of some other entity taking action. But this can be misleading. What happens is that the *people* of the churches do something, or the *members* of the Senate, or the *individuals* that form a group. It is clear, therefore, that you cannot raise the social level unless you raise it through the individual.

After all, this has always been the case. And besides this, there is the pioneer, the enterprising individual. No reform, no correction of an evil, no advance of any kind in all the annals of history was ever begun without an individual to get it started.

When the fires of the American Revolution were burning low and men watched the flame of its hope go down towards the ashes of despair, how were those fires rekindled? Who breathed them back into life? Was it the Continental Congress? Did someone appoint a Committee on Unrevolutionary Activities? Was it an ecclesiastical commission? We know the answer. It was an individual theretofore obscure, or almost so, Tom Paine, whom George Washington credited with saving the Revolution.

Who, in the nineteenth century, reformed the prisons and established humane treatment for the insane? Was it an outcry from the clergy? An impassioned plea by the medical profession? A committee of prominent citizens who put an advertisement in the newspapers? No, it was a relatively unknown girl from Hampden, Maine, Dorothea Dix.

Who got the American public school system going? Did someone arise in the House of Representatives and declare with his fist pounding his desk that a great Nation deserved an educated citizenry, whereupon the House of Representatives, instantly persuaded by such impeccable logic, unanimously voted both an authorization and an appropriation, and the Senate declared itself mortified because it had not thought of it first? No, it was a lone enthusiast, a Massachusetts lawyer named Horace Mann, who did, incidentally, arrive after a while in the House of Representatives.

And so we might continue with name after name. Christianity was not established by people of prominence, people who wielded influence and who had evolved a plan to save the world. Jesus of Nazareth was an individual. So was the Apostle, Paul, and so were the people who formed those early Christian congregations.

When anyone asks, how much does the individual count? surely the first of the answers is this: it depends —and always must—upon the individual. If you have the conviction, the courage, the patience and the persistence, and if you are willing to put everything you have into the venture, win or lose, you can go immense distances, in this time or any other, as an individual.

But still, it may be objected, these that we have mentioned were after all outstanding people. They had unusual talent, conspicuous ability—or at any rate they had a sort of boldness that the majority cannot claim. "Say something, Mr. Preacher, that applies to John Doe or even to Caspar Milquetoast!" None of *us*, of course, admit to being John Does, and certainly none of us are Caspar Milquetoasts; but still we know a lot of people who *are*—one or the other. People who are timid—who don't in the least want to save the world but just want to buy a television set. What do they count for as individuals?

I will answer frankly. At present, not much! Caspar Milquetoast is an appealing little figure and it's natural to be sorry for him. But just the same, he is responsible for a large part of what is the matter with us. He reads the wrong newspapers, believes lies, follows his prejudices, wraps himself up in his fears. And worst of all, he doesn't know when to be angry.

That is one of the truly serious things that has happened to the multitude of so-called ordinary people. They have forgotten how to be indignant. This is not because they are overflowing with human kindness but because they are morally soft and compliant. When they see evil and injustice, they are pained but not revolted. They mutter and mumble; they never cry out. They commit the sin of not being angry.

Yet, their anger is the one thing above all others that would make them count. If they cannot lead crusades, or initiate reforms, they can at least create the conditions in which crusades can be effectual and reforms successful. The wrath of the multitude could bring back decency and integrity into public life; it could frighten the corrupt demagogue into silence and blast the rumormonger into oblivion. It could give honest leaders a chance to win. If

the multitude of ordinary people would rise up in righteous indignation and let the sound of their anger be heard,
we should no longer have to read in the newspapers of a
district attorney, flouted by criminals, who puts his head
in his arms and weeps; or of a Senator who groans aloud
when his motives are distorted in careless debate and the
toil of weeks is heedlessly cast aside. Nor of a hundred
other things of which these two are representative.

It is frequently said that there are no longer good
leaders: men and women with the force of character, the
mentality, the vision, the integrity to steer us through
the dangerous waters all around us and the storms ahead.
I am not so sure that this is true. I think it should be put
as a question, not stated as a fact. I am doubtful, very
doubtful, whether good leadership is as widely welcomed
as it used to be; and whether it is recognized when it
appears.

But however this may be, leadership in a free country
is not rulership; nor is there any ruling class. Leadership
must emerge from the people. People who believe that the
individual counts must produce the outstanding individual—and then help him to count. He is their agent, their
representative. Only as such individuals emerge and are
encouraged and supported, can a society based on individual significance maintain its special character, and only
so can it endure. It is indispensable that all of us together
provide the conditions under which we shall be well and
wisely led. And as I said before, this means that at least
we must be willing to be angry—at lies and cheating,
venality and corruption; at least, we must stand up for
common decency. If we will not do that much, what hope
can there be for us? What good are we? Why should God
or history preserve us? Why should we be saved?

But besides regaining the capacity for righteous indignation, the individual—whoever he is, and no matter how anonymous—can exert continuously, and indeed, *must* exert continuously, the entire influence of his life and character. There is not one of us who does not every day appreciably affect our total situation. Individuals are every hour making a difference in other individuals and therefore in all of us. By the stand we take—or refuse to take—in ordinary conversation, we encourage either the true or the false, the good or the bad; we make it either easier or harder for other people to have courage, to deepen their convictions, to make right choices.

It is out of the vast complex of the relationships of individuals that the impulse comes to raise our standards—or the willingness to let them drop. When we express our own prejudices we deepen prejudice in others. When we counter them, prejudice everywhere receives a setback. If we stand by our convictions, gently but firmly refusing to be intimidated, either to please a friend or placate an enemy, conviction finds a stronger rootage. It is not necessary to be too much bothered by the things that people *say* at such a time, the irritation or annoyance they express. Something has happened within them that they could not prevent; something that, whether they wished it or not, made them believe more deeply that character is a reality, that there are things in life to respect.

How much does the individual count? It is a question that he himself must answer, that all must answer, each by the manner of his life.

13

What May We Depend Upon?

WITHIN AN astonishingly short space of time, a world that seemed secure has become surrounded with uncertainties. What is there that we may depend upon?

Certainly not the physical fabric of our civilization, for we have seen already how swiftly it can be destroyed. What has happened in other places can happen also to our own abodes. The stone and iron, the bricks and mortar, the wood and brass of which our cities are composed might vanish in a cloud of dust. So might our bank accounts, our stocks and bonds, our symbols of material substance. If we survived at all, it might be on a very elemental level, one for which we are unfitted and unprepared. This is not a prospect that invites repose.

But as well as the physical danger, there is the widespread loss of confidence in what we have learned to call *intangibles*. The intangible of *faith*—faith in ourselves and in our destiny. The intangible of *meaning*—in human life and in the universe. The intangible of *sanity*—in a world careening towards the madness of preventable disaster. Even the intangible of *common sense*—mocked by the nonsense statesmen shout at one another in assemblies. What has happened to these intangibles, upon which we thought we could depend?

Everything seems to have become unsettled and uncertain. Not only the physical fabric of our civilization, but the moral force beneath it, too. Nor can we exempt the scientific and the rational, for after mastering one of the most cryptic problems of the universe, the secret of the atom, we find the solution pointing a dagger at our hearts, our scientific progress suddenly become a terrifying apparition, threatening us with catastrophe.

What may we depend upon? What may we believe in? What can we assume as true while we try to think our way through these enigmas, puzzles and conundrums? Is there any ground beneath our feet? Anything solid to hold on to during setbacks and disappointments? Anything upon the basis of which we can renew our courage, take heart and proceed?

Well, if we want a genuine answer, one that does not obscure the facts or try to sentimentalize away realities, we can scarcely do better than consider the following words of Emerson's. They are not immediately comforting, and that is a part of their merit, for instant solace is seldom lasting. "Nothing is secure," says Emerson, "but life, transition, the energizing spirit. No love can be bound by oath or covenant to secure it against a higher love. No truth so sublime but it may be trivial tomorrow in the light of new thoughts. People wish to be settled; only so far as they are *unsettled* is there any hope . . ." And then he quotes Oliver Cromwell, who said, "A man never rises so high as when he knows not whither he is going."

As I have indicated, there is little reassurance in these words when first we read them. The quotation from Cromwell, particularly, appears to have but little substance. If a man never rises so high as when he knows not whither he is going, most men nowadays should be sailing through the stratosphere. For if ever there was a time when men did not know where they were going, that time is now. And yet, how high have they risen? This, I said to myself when I came upon the saying, is just not true. Men do not know where they are going and yet instead of rising higher they are sinking lower than they were before.

Then I began to reflect a little. After all, Cromwell was no fool. He must have meant something definite, something that made sense, even if it was not immediately self-evident. I recalled some history. I remembered that Columbus was a man who after a while became uncertain where he was going. His original expectation disappointed him. But he went on sailing. And not only did his voyage bring success but he rose to higher stature in the course of it. I thought of others. The figure of Jesus came before my mind, agonizing in the Garden of Gethsemane, no longer sure where he was going. But who can doubt his stature or the height of his achievement?

"A man never rises so high as when he knows not whither he is going!" It could be true. It could be true in spite of contradictions. The people of the modern world, some of them, have sunk to a very low level. But those who have sunk the lowest have been the ones who shouted to the rest of us that they were surest that they knew where they were going. They were going to dominate the earth; they were going to crush and trample until they had reduced us all to slavery. They were going to establish a new and barbarous tyranny, one that would last a thousand years.

These were the ones who sank the lowest: these who said that they were sure. And now the new threat—what is it but the same thing? The sureness of the Nazis is followed by the sureness of the communists; they, too, are sure that they will dominate the earth. And see how low they are sinking.

Perhaps there is something in this saying of Cromwell's, the truth of which does not instantly appear. Perhaps the people, millions of them, who are called upon today as they never were before to make great efforts, great changes, great sacrifices, are among the people who do not know where they are going. They wish that their leaders would speak to them more plainly; they would like to know much better than they do what goal they are aiming at, what destination they can hope to reach. Meanwhile, however, somewhere beneath their disappointment and dismay, somewhere below anxieties and fears, they do have a sense of direction; and they feel at times as though they have the courage for it, the willingness to venture. Could it happen that these voiceless millions could rise to new heights, new levels of achievement, even though the way be difficult and the labors of the journey arduous?

We think our age unusual in not knowing whither it is going. But did the Greeks know in the age of Pericles? Or Europe in the Renaissance? Or the United States in the eighteenth century? We certainly need new concepts —new and greater; and we need clearer programs, less ambiguous policies, and a stronger, warmer faith to give them impulse. But perhaps the one thing that we *cannot* know—cannot know as we would like to know it—is where we are going; perhaps it is only the direction that can be plainly seen.

If so, Cromwell may not have been wrong. One of the things to place reliance upon may be the belief that somehow, because of the nature of the venture, we shall come to higher levels. Certainly, on lower levels we could not even survive. So rise we must. For only a nobler humanity could be equal to our present problems. Only a higher level can be sufficient to the task. This, then, may be the beginning of an answer: that no matter what the harshness of our situation, no matter what its pain and loss, it is the necessary condition of our advance: that it *requires* us to advance. Perhaps this is something believable, something that we may depend upon.

Yes, but if so, it does not bring us much security. Certainly not in the sense that shelters our own hopes, or is protective of our habitations, or defends us against the onslaughts of adversity. Concerning all that, however, Emerson, who quoted the Cromwell saying, is quite explicit. None of these things *can* be secure. "Nothing is secure," he says, "but life, transition, the energizing spirit."

And it is there that we come face to face with a new scale of values. If we suppose that the purpose of the universe is to serve our personal wishes, we have misconceived the matter from the start. If we think that God should be the guarantee of all that is precious to us and should defend us from the chance of loss or dispossession, we are still children spiritually. We have not even begun to know what religion is. For religion is not intended to make God the servant of man, but man the servant of God. The great purposes of life can never be subordinate to our personal aims; our personal aims must serve life's purposes.

This is one of the hardest matters with which an interpreter of religion can ever try to deal. It is not hard because the question itself is difficult. It is hard because so many people are accustomed only to a childish point of view. Many times in my ministry I have felt directed against me the finger of a deprived person's accusation because this person felt unjustly treated by the God I am supposed to represent. Such an individual becomes resentful at religion, and resentful against a minister because he is a representative of what the individual thinks has harmed him. It is as though he should say, "I have no further use for your religion. I have no further use for your Boss; he has not treated me right, he has let me down."

That is the way such people think of God: as a sort of boss of the universe who assumes contractual obligations in return for being worshipped. All of which is misconceived and utterly mistaken! It comes from childish ideas which, instead of allowing religion to arise from the real, turn it into a shelter from reality. The fact is that God makes no bargains with anybody, and, in the sense implied, he has no representatives. The business of a church, and therefore of a preacher, is not to make unauthorized promises on behalf of the Deity, but to persuade people to grow up spiritually. What people need, as over against what they want, is to be brought nearer to the purposes of God and in the service of these purposes to grow to the fullness of their human stature, seeking no shelter that will shrink their souls.

What may we depend upon? It can certainly never be the hope that God will make life easy for us; or that he will even protect us from grief and loss. "Nothing is secure," says Emerson, "but life, transition, the energizing spirit." If we would find a solid standing for our feet, therefore, we must give up the immature and illusory and accept our role as the servants of life, the agents of transition, the children of the energizing spirit.

"No love can be bound by oath or covenant to secure it against a higher love," Emerson continues. "No truth so sublime but it may be trivial tomorrow in the light of new thoughts." Yes, even love and truth in any of their special manifestations are transitory. No individual truth must be

loved more than truth itself. And nothing to which the
heart is drawn must hold the heart against a higher loyalty. "People wish," concludes Emerson, "to be settled;
only so far as they are unsettled is there any hope."

As soon as we view our situation with detachment—
detachment, I mean, from selfish and self-centered aims—
we can see how true this is. There would be no advance
whatever if people became settled. "Let us stay here,"
said the intimate disciples of Jesus on the Mount of
Transfiguration. "Let us build Temples." They wanted to
settle down forever with the mountain-top experience.
This that we now have, they said, should last always. But
they were mistaken. Jesus insisted upon leading his disciples down the mountainside into the problems and vexa-
tions of his uncompleted mission, which were waiting for
them in the valleys and on the plains.

That is the way it always is and always must be. Only
so far as we are *un*settled is there any hope. If we of this
age were settled, the injustices of the world would go on
indefinitely and the wretched would remain in their
squalor and misery. We would pity them but never turn a
hand to help them to a fuller share in human life. So it
would be with everything else. We *need* the conditions
that unsettle us. Only so far as we are *un*settled is there
any hope! When we have stretched our hearts to understand it, this is something to depend upon! It means that
moral requirements are real and that they must prevail.
Unsettlement continues until they do prevail. Our unsettlement is itself the evidence for moral law in the universe, a testimony for God.

It is the same with the battles of truth with falsehood.
Lies can succeed only for a time. The reason is very
simple. Truth is concerned with *what is really so*. And

what is *not* really so will always in the end defeat its followers and adherents. If someone says that a certain path does *not* lead to a precipice and it actually does, those who follow that path will discover the precipice—and therefore the lie. It may be a costly discovery: it depends upon how fast they are moving when they make it. But there is no question at all about truth revealing itself, or about the unsettlement that always goes with lies.

The fact is that the more we go into the matter, the more sure it is that moral factors rule our destiny. It will not be evident so long as we are thinking chiefly of ourselves, setting up our own enjoyments, our own ambitions, as the final test of value in the universe. But as soon as we stop being spiritual infants crying to be comforted, and begin to look at life from a maturer viewpoint, we see that all the final values are secure.

This is our starting-point, the only one that can get us going in the right direction when we look for what we may depend upon in the world of today and tomorrow. Gradually, as we come to understand it, we begin to have a deepening faith in the meaning of life. We feel the growth of courage, and presently a deep and strengthening contentment. We are finding what there is—and *really* is—to depend upon. From this, a great deal else can take its rise. Confidence and buoyancy, for instance. Nobody can be truly buoyant who is too much attached to his own concerns. Indeed, a good deal of the gloominess of what passes for faith is due to the fact that those who cling to it are also clinging to their own littleness, and they hope somehow to buy God off, to get him on the side of their pettiness. They are prisoners of small aims and they want God to preside over their prison. This he will never do.

Religion, if it is real, is big. As big as a summer sky or a winter storm. As big as a garden of flowers or a Garden of Gethsemane. As big as a world that is dying and a world that is waiting to be born. It is when we discover this that we find something to depend upon; and when we find it, nothing can take it away.

14

Invitation to Serenity

SERENITY, tranquillity, peace—these have always been words men have loved to hear spoken. Even the sound of them is reassuring, at any rate for the passing moment, so that no matter how well we remember the disappointments of the past, we feel a fleeting sense of hope revived. Perhaps there *is* such a thing as serenity. But where do you find it?

And that, of course—if one may use the rather mercenary term so popular in current parlance—is the "sixty-four dollar question." Certainly, it is a very remunerative question, for what question has been more exploited? Who can count the books and articles, bright, crisp, readable, and as shallow as dew, written on this subject to a profitable formula?

Then, too, I remember some years ago receiving a multigraphed communication from an agency that offered me peace of mind for one dollar a year. It seemed like a bargain. In case I did not have a dollar, the agency would promptly send me a little cardboard bank in which I could save a dollar up, a dime at a time. Perhaps it was the thoughtfulness of this arrangement that predisposed me to read the entire communication. At any rate, I read it. And this is what I found: that I can know exactly what to do in every situation, and how to do it perfectly, for God in the midst of me will be my intelligence. That is to say, he will if I send this institution a dollar a year.

Once I am thus equipped, the letter goes on, I shall enjoy unprecedented peace of mind, and therefore be able to solve my problems easily, think constructively, and live harmoniously.

Nor is this all! Gradually, as I get my dollar's worth of guidance, I shall find that I have reached a condition in which I have no room for problems! Being entirely filled up with solutions, my serenity will be complete. All that I need do is check which payment plan I prefer: a dollar right away or after I have saved it up in the little cardboard bank. And the letter closes by saying that the institution blesses me in Christ's name.

All of which has a certain charm about it, and one cannot be absolutely certain that the proprietors of such an institution consider themselves frauds. After all, they promise very little more than a good many other institutions, both sacred and secular, and some of them quite respectable—and they promise it at a much fairer price! As for the fact that they cannot deliver what they offer, neither can these other institutions, even though they, too, may presume to bless us in Christ's name.

That, however, is not our chief concern, and I mention it here only because it illustrates so perfectly the mass appeal of the question we are considering. We might classify the appeal at this level as serenity for the dollar-a-year market.

But let us look at the same question at another level. Where do you get serenity? In 1935, a very interesting book appeared, written by Edmund Jacobson, M.D., called *You Must Relax*. It was a popular version of a more technical book by Dr. Jacobson, which had reported his research into neuromuscular tensions and their role in disease and everyday life. Unquestionably, the more technical version was a very useful book, especially to physicians who needed to treat cases of neurotic fatigue in their patients.

But what of the popular version? It, too, I think, had a certain amount of merit. Dr. Jacobson's suggestions for inducing tranquillity through physical relaxation might very well be given consideration. It should be noted, also, that Dr. Jacobson does not promise for this method all that some of his readers may suppose. Except at moments, he writes with a physician's caution. But just the same, his book does not reach the real problem. No matter how good his method may have been—or still be, for that matter—considered as a physical supplement to other approaches, it could never solve the basic problem. For the fact is—and I think it is quite an obvious fact—that serenity is seldom lost from physical causes, and physical remedies cannot supply what is wanting.

I mention this book, not to attack it, but for the same reason that I mentioned the multigraphed letter: it illustrates, although at a more rational level, the widespread desire to find serenity without an arduous search, and *to possess it on some simple, easy basis.* In the first case, the basis was self-hypnosis through superstition; in the second, it was exaggerated claims for a physical therapy. Both, in their own way, manifest the same illusion, namely, that a relaxed state of mind can be achieved without mastering the conditions that cause the tensions. Each promises a short cut, a more or less effortless and easy way to well-being and serenity.

This, I am afraid, is characteristic of most of the methods that promise serenity. If we examined them, one by one, I think we could come to no other conclusion. We would notice, again and again, that the popular appeal is based upon the hope that there exists an easy way. And our verdict would have to be that *there is no easy way*. Consequently, all these invitations to serenity would have to be counted in the end as disappointing.

At this point, a good many of us—unfortunately—cease to inquire. We give up the quest. There *is* no path to serenity, we say. But here we have run ahead of the evidence. What we have found is not that serenity is unattainable, but that it is not *easily* attainable—which is a quite different thing. And the recognition of this difference should inspire some further questions.

We should ask, for instance, whether there *should* be peace of mind on a simple or easy basis. If we are disinclined to consider this question in the context of morality and the higher levels of religion because we think we are familiar with their admonitions, perhaps we would be willing to consider it in the context of science.

If so, we might turn to a recent essay by Julian Huxley, presented together with a lecture by his famous grandfather, Thomas Huxley, in a book called *Touchstone for Ethics*. Both the Huxleys, each in his own generation, are rather rigorous logicians, and their devotion to the scientific method is beyond dispute. Yet they tell us, each in his own way, that conflict is essential to the human mind; that without it, we should never have acquired mentality at all—not to mention ethics.

Conflict, they assure us, is the condition of progress. Without conflict—the conflict of ideas, of aims, of purposes—within the mind of man, we would still be less than human. It is the antagonism of alternatives that forces us to choose. Little by little, each hard-won choice builds up in society and in the individuals it molds, certain ethical requirements. These requirements are not something marginal, something on the edge of life: they are its very essence. Without them, we could not be human at all. And as human societies develop, the requirements grow.

Indeed, we should put it the other way around and say that because the requirements grow, human societies develop. When, for instance, barbarian practices are given up, such as the practice of murdering a stranger on sight, it is the result of struggle: a struggle within the mind as well as within the society because a new alternative has been presented. Gradually, this new alternative, which in the example we are using, would be treating the stranger with consideration instead of killing him, sets up new and powerful tensions. The old practice comes to seem wrong, the new alternative right. Or in other words, while the force of tradition is behind the prevailing practice, the attraction of a new attitude stands in vigorous opposition to it. This means that every time the barbarian kills a stranger on sight he feels a sense of guilt. Ultimately, this feeling of guiltiness becomes so strong that it is essential to get rid of it. Perhaps for a while the barbarian makes a sacrifice to his gods and cleanses himself through a ritual act from his blood-guiltiness. But eventually, this fails to relieve the tension. The only way to get rid of the guilty feeling is to stop killing strangers.

So this choice begins to be made, and through it the barbarian is lifted to a higher level. By hundreds and thousands of such choices, civilization is slowly built up. And the civilized man comes to have, instead of barbarian customs and tabus, a strongly entrenched discernment of right and wrong—or, more simply, a civilized conscience.

That, very briefly, is the scientific approach to this question. It discloses that conflict is essential to the human level, and it implies that the conflict must inevitably be ethical.

This being so, how is serenity possible except where ethical conditions are fulfilled? Or, in simplest language, how can you have peace of mind unless you do what is right? Your situation, at your own higher level, is just like that of the barbarian. Instead of sacrifices to the gods, or performing other ritual acts, you invent rationalizations and excuses—though sometimes, of course, you do seek forgiveness by a ritual act. But you can no more succeed in getting rid of your tensions by this method than the barbarian could. The conflict will tear you apart—and will keep on doing so until you change your behavior. In short, you cannot have serenity cheaply. You will have to accept its conditions.

And notice! I am meeting the question on a modern-minded, scientific basis. I have made no appeal to religious authority. I have referred only to Julian and Thomas Huxley. It is interesting, especially to those of us who grew up with modern psychology, to observe the way in which people think they have escaped the ethical by giving up religion for science—or what they think is science—whereas they are more torn by moral conflict than they ever were before.

For instance, some years ago, an acquaintance who had come to me for counsel, and after receiving it had rejected it, went on my advice to see a psychiatrist. After a few weeks he came back and told me that I had recommended the wrong psychiatrist. What he needed, he said, was a *restful* psychiatrist!

How completely he revealed himself in that remark! As, of course, a sick soul always does. Honest psychiatry was making the same demands upon him that honest religion was. It could not be otherwise, for both are governed by the realities of human nature. These realities were requiring that he change his attitude, revise the aims of his life, and because he refused to do so, he was full of inner conflict.

Psychiatry could no more give him a cheap escape from this state of conflict than religion could; to get peace of mind, the man would have to make the choices and accept the purposes that *provided* peace of mind. Or, to use more simple words, he could not *do* wrong and *feel* right, and that is what he wanted. By a "restful psychiatrist," he meant one who would charm away his feeling of guilt and make him feel well without being cured. It was impossible. Just as impossible as that water should flow uphill. It was against realities—against natural law, the law of human nature.

So we come to this, then: that serenity is possible only when the right choices are made, the difficult choices, the demanding ones, the choices which are attracting you in spite of yourself, and attracting you so powerfully that you are kept in a state of tension, a state of inner conflict. You cannot choose the lower against the higher and have peace of mind. What you will have is inner turmoil.

The same conflict and unrest that are manifest in the individual are afflicting our entire civilization: afflicting it because it refuses to make this choice. We see the evidence of it in every issue of the daily newspaper. Not only unhappy people—individuals—who refuse this demand, but unhappy governments, unhappy congresses and parliaments, unhappy political parties, trying to feel right while they are doing wrong. So that they lose not only serenity, but even dignity—and at times, all but the barest residues of self-respect.

But chiefly, I want to emphasize the individual, the individual who is, and quite inevitably, a member of society and a part of the social process in which he is involved. And I would like to say something at this point that it seems very hard for people to understand, though, if they would really think about it, they would understand it very well. People sometimes say to me, "When I go to church, I feel entitled to be comforted. I need it. I don't need stimulation. I get that every day of the week. I want peace of mind."

Sometimes, they ask me if I don't think there is sufficient solace in beauty and that religion should comfort the heart with it. They are even kind enough to suggest that when I wish to do it, I can myself convey some of this beauty in a sermon, and they mean—I'm sorry to say so, but this is what they *do* mean—that I might convey beauty and solace without involving anything ethical— without challenging the conscience. In this way, they show the symptoms of the moral sickness that afflicts our age.

Now, the answer is a very straightforward one. I have had a lot of practice in making sermons, and probably I can make a sermon out of almost anything. Just as an experienced sculptor can do something creditable with almost any piece of stone, or a practiced musician could develop something acceptable out of any theme that happened to be offered to him. Probably, I could do very nearly what these people want. And I love the beautiful. Everything beautiful has a powerful attraction for me, music, art, poetry, all of it. I am overjoyed when I can find a single day—just one whole day—in which I can go out and look at the spring, just look at it, before it passes into summer. Beauty, to me, is an intensity of emotion that is often indescribable. So I know what these people are talking about—sometimes, I am afraid, even better than they do.

Indeed, if I am to make a personal confession, I think I must say that the love of beauty is my only real temptation. The loveliness of life, convertible in so many ways into so many lovely things, has always had a powerful influence on me. And what I feel, of course, can be converted into words. It can turn sermons into sedatives—rather refined sedatives—with God in them, and Jesus in them, and all the apostles, saints and martyrs, everyone of them on your side—and all of them transformed into opium: not religion, the opium of the common people, but religion, the sedative of superior souls.

Yes, and souls that whether superior or otherwise, are thereby betrayed! Betrayed just as truly on this level as on any grosser one. Because they have been helped towards their own undoing.

No, to those who ask that we should preach on solace, some of us can only answer that we do so every time we preach. A sermon calling for righteousness is a sermon invoking serenity—on the only terms upon which serenity may be achieved. Every appeal is an appeal to accept the peace of God—the peace of God which cannot be had except by those who have chosen righteousness—the righteousness that calls to them with all the force and vigor of the present day. And of course it is the same with other things than sermons. It is the same always, and everywhere. These are the conditions of spiritual life.

I do not say that even then—when a soul accepts what righteousness requires—the conflict will be over. We still grow by conflict and we always must. But I do say that there comes to be something untroubled and secure *at the center of life.* Something that grows more confident, more tranquil, more at rest within itself. It cannot be disturbed from the outside, and as long as its choices remain the true ones, it cannot be *deeply* disturbed from within.

This, it seems to me, is just what Jesus meant by the most famous invitation to serenity that history records. "Come unto me," he said, "and I will give you rest. Take my yoke upon you, and learn of me, for I am meek and lowly in heart: and ye shall find rest unto your souls. For my yoke is easy, and my burden light."

Few passages in the Bible have been more often misinterpreted—expounded as a mere offer to soothe away weariness, or a divine promise of relaxed requirements. How far it is from the truth! "*Learn* of me," Jesus said; and "take my *yoke* upon you." What is a yoke? It is itself a burden, but a means of carrying other and heavier burdens more easily. As a figure of speech, it means a discipline, an acceptance of a requirement laid upon us, the requirement of doing right, by means of which all other burdens and requirements grow lighter and easier to be borne.

"For I am meek and lowly in heart," Jesus continued. Not rebellious and mutinous, but adjusted to what the soul demands. Accepting the realities that mold a life to goodness, and sometimes to greatness, through lowliness of heart. Follow my way, says Jesus—and his whole life shows what way it is—and you shall find rest unto your souls. "For my yoke is easy and my burden light."

Easy? Yes, for when you follow this way, the yoke fits on your shoulders without chafing and the burden does not wear you down. Or to set aside the metaphor, you are no longer fighting the higher claims of your own life. Instead, you are releasing your strength to carry your burdens. And that is what rest is—strength, not weakness; and serenity is possible in other ways because you have the strength of its rest in your soul.

The phrase to notice, however, and the phrase that is all too little noticed in this invitation of Jesus to find inward rest, is "learn of me." He made no promise of inward peace on light or easy conditions. "Make your choices as I make mine," he was saying. "Discover what I turn aside from and what I accept. Learn the power of righteousness. It is a secret but an open secret. Anyone can possess it who really wants it. It's even rather simple in the end. You just give up pretending, give up excusing, give up the subtleties with which you have tried so hard to keep yourself deceived, and call right, right, and follow it. When in doubt, make sure that you are not being deceived—self-deceived—and do the best you know. If you find yourself mistaken, admit it, repent it, and change your course of action without hesitation. Get accustomed to doing right—but without being self-righteous. Do it as the "meek and lowly in heart" do it.

Begin along these lines and the tensions will slacken. You will still have conflicts but they will not tear you apart. Instead of your energy being dissipated in a hopeless struggle against truth and righteousness, it will become available—fully available for living your life. You will have serenity, "rest to your soul."

Then you will know a kind of solace you did not realize existed. The loveliness of life will come to you without effort. Instead of seeking beauty to hide the ugliness you fear to see—or to reveal—you will see beauty growing and actually transforming ugliness. You will know why "Solomon in all his glory" was not as beautiful as "the lilies of the field," the unforced, natural loveliness of life.

And your fears will melt away. Even those fears that you never mention—very rarely mention even to yourself. They melt away. Because nothing alarming can finally touch you. Knowing the inner reality of the spiritual, you know what it means: that all final things are secure. This is a kind of faith you cannot have by arguing yourself into it. It comes only by experience, and only by the kind of experience that lies on the other side of this surrender: the surrender to righteousness, and the power of it. It is a power that presently becomes a glory, too. Sometimes an austere glory, but sometimes a tenderness and sweetness of the soul unutterable. So that you know in the only way it can be known that God lives—lives because your own soul lives. That is the evidence. What a sad thing it is that the world is so full of half-alive souls, all asking whether God is less alive than they are! Until the soul lives, God is a far-away mystery, a question that cannot be answered. But when the soul is alive, so is everything. And instead of asking "Where is God?" you ask, "Where is he not?" And when you can say that, God will not be far away: and neither will serenity.

III

And Thus to Venture

THE CHAPEL *of Staunton Harold, in Lei-
cestershire, England, was built in the seven-*
teenth century, when civil war had ravaged
*the land and all hope everywhere was at its
lowest ebb. On one of the walls of the chapel
will be found a tablet bearing this inscription:*
*"In the year 1653, when all things were
throughout the nation either demollisht or
profaned, Sir Robert Shirley, Barronet,
founded this church: Whose singular praise
it is to have done the best things in the worst
times and hoped them in the most calami-
tous."*

15

The Path to Spiritual Maturity

ONE OF THE MOST tenacious hopes that human beings entertain is that of discovering some principle of religion or philosophy which will reduce the complexities of their lives to complete simplicity. They cannot give up believing that somewhere in the universe, if they could only find it, is a master-key that opens all doors by turning it in the lock.

Sometimes they think this master-key is a "rule of life" that can be applied quite simply and directly to every kind of problem with the certainty of providing an infallible solution. Sometimes they think of it as supernatural guidance, very clear and detailed, which they think should be available whenever requested according to the prescribed formula. In the past, this sort of guidance was often sought for in the Bible, and some of the claims made for it bordered on the sacrilegious.

There is the once popular story, for instance, of the lady who had turned her lavender gown so that the inside surface of the cloth would be on the outside and thus give it a new-looking appearance. After a while, however, this side became even more faded and worn than the original outer surface, so the question was, should she turn the cloth inside out once more or dye it black? Which would be better? Deeply perplexed, she took the problem to her Bible. After praying for a moment, she opened the pages at random and, looking down, her glance fell upon the verse, "Turn again, why will ye die?" Trusting in the phonetics rather than the spelling, she took this to be a precise instruction and her gown was turned again and remained lavender. As to whether the Bible really contains such a verse, bibliolaters did not stop to inquire. Nor were they dismayed by satire: they smiled but found the story satisfying.

Where the expectation has been lost that religion can supply the magic "rule of life," people turn to a political axiom or an economic panacea, or they join the communists and follow the "party line." Or they may turn to the newest psychological trick, as they did to auto-suggestion in the nineteen-twenties, or to some exotic kind of mysticism which they hope will insulate them from their problems altogether.

What they are looking for—and in the interest of un-mistakable clarity, this perhaps should be emphasized—is not a general principle or code of ethics which can be *thoughtfully* applied to their problems, and with a step-by-step awareness of the pitfalls; but an *automatic* rule. To return, for instance, to the case of the Bible, they do not seek the guidance that comes from a careful study of its contents, but an instant, verbalistic command in the random picking of a text. 'Party line' guidance is but little different: no matter what the inconsistencies within the process as a whole, or even the downright contradictions, what you follow is a day-by-day direction as to what you must think and do.

Diagnostically, of course, we can refer this attitude to arrested emotional development, and this is so no matter which of the 'master-keys' is adopted and irrespective of whether it is religious. It is an attempt to return emotion-ally to childhood when the parent answered baffling ques-

tions and took over bothersome situations by giving
directions as to what must be done. If there was doubt as
to a course of action, it could be resolved by saying,
"Mother tells me to do thus and so, and Mother is always
right." Adults who retain this attitude or long to restore it
are not really grown up. They are in search of a 'rule of
life' to take the place of the mother, or a 'party line' (or
the like) as a substitute for the authority of the father.
Just as they said, "Mother is always right," so they want
to say that their 'rule of life' is always right, or their psychological trick, or their 'party line,' or whatever it is that
they try to depend upon. And if they turn to an escapist
sort of mysticism and try to fly away from their problems
entirely, what they are doing is seeking a substitute for
the solace of the mother's arms.

For the fact is that there *is* no 'master-key' or 'rule of
life' in the sense that would satisfy the spiritually immature. Even the Golden Rule of the New Testament,
which, with its counterparts in the other great religions,*
is probably the most condensed statement of ethical wisdom ever achieved, is far from automatic in its applications. "Whatsoever ye would that men should do to you,
do ye even so to them," seems not too difficult at times in
personal situations—not difficult, that is, in seeing how to
apply it; persuading ourselves to do what it asks may be
extremely strenuous. But even in personal situations, it is
often hard to know what *truly* would be reciprocity. A
parent, for instance, cannot always do what his children
wish he would do, or what they would do in his place, or

* The Buddhist and Confucian "Golden Rules" are the same as that
of the New Testament except that they express the principle with a
negative emphasis: "Do not unto others as ye would not that others
should do unto you."

even what he would like them to do if the roles were reversed. The question of wisdom enters, and of the differences between sorts of persons, some of whom in a given situation would act in one way and some in others.

Let us use an illustration. A young man wants permission to leave home and to be financed while seeking his fortune in a distant city. His father believes that he himself at this boy's age could have managed such an adventure very well, so on the basis of a simple reciprocity he ought to give permission. The fact is, however, that the young man is not nearly as responsible a person as his father was at his age and is likely to do badly. The father must thus reflect that if he *were* the boy, constituted as this boy actually is, he would ultimately be grateful—or at least *should* be—if permission were denied. To the father, this becomes the application of the Golden Rule—but not to the son!

But let us move away from purely personal applications and inquire, for instance, as to how this Rule can be applied to two nations or groups of nations at the same time if they are violently hostile to each other and have opposed objectives? Or, to take up an actual case, how could we have applied it, in the simple and direct sense that many people like to think is possible, in the Europe of the nineteen-thirties? We wanted to be left in peace; it was therefore our obligation to leave others in peace. So we left Germany in peace. We did to Hitler as we hoped he would do to us. But what did we do to the Austria that Hitler annexed? Or to the Czechoslovakia he occupied? Did we leave them in peace or did we leave them in chains? Did we act towards them as we would have liked them to act towards us?

I am not saying, of course, that the Golden Rule is incapable of application. I believe the exact contrary. What I am saying is that it cannot be *simply* or *automatically* applied. Neither this rule nor any other can relieve us of the burden of difficult decisions which we must think through for ourselves. The requirement laid upon us—and it is a perfectly reasonable one—is that we shall use the minds God gave us, and for the purpose for which they were given. In doing this, there is a great deal that can help us: all that the great teachers and exemplars have bequeathed to us, all that the saints and sages have bestowed upon us. But none of this help is magical or automatic. It will not support an immature and childish attitude.

The fact is that no dependence upon the magical and superstitious can release us—or *should* release us—from the pain and labor of understanding our own problems. It is by this pain and labor that we grow in character and are able at last to prove equal to our problems. Whenever it seems that we have escaped from this necessity, we can be sure that before long two things will have happened to us: first, we shall have become lesser persons, too morally cowardly to be sufficient to the claims upon us, and second, that realities will catch up with us.

There were people a little while since who thought world peace could be preserved through trusting in a magic formula. Irrespective of whether nations were just and observed the laws of human rights, if they were "peace-loving" they could join together in establishing a world government, a much stronger world government than the United Nations, with the compromises of which they were much dissatisfied. Some of these nations—one in particular—oppressed and enslaved their own people and had aggressive designs against other peoples. "No matter!" said these believers in the magic formula, "the point is that these nations are 'peace-loving.'" And so they thought that peace could be built upon injustice and tyranny, condoning even aggressive ambition, and not come tumbling down upon them. They refused to think candidly, they turned away from moral obligation, they closed their eyes to reality. Chanting their formula, they insisted that all would be well. They declared that God was with them since God is on the side of peace. But what happened was that their own moral level was depressed, and then, when they had weakened themselves by escapism, reality caught up with them. If not before, it caught up with them with Korea.

Let us understand, then, that in personal life and in public affairs alike, the childish attitude must be outgrown. We must take the path that leads to spiritual maturity. Rules of life and maxims, master-keys and magic formulas all are unavailing. We *must* use the minds that God gave us. Why should he relieve us of this obligation? Does the wise mother tell her grown children exactly what they must think and do? The mother who dominates her children in this way makes emotional cripples of them—and all of us who have tried to encourage these cripples to get up on their feet and walk know how serious their injuries can be. All too many people, unhappily, want a God who is a domineering mother; tender, yes—like their own mothers—tender but domineering. Quite clearly, God declines this role. There is nothing in experience, plainly and honestly looked at, that justifies the thought that he has ever taken it. He wants us to grow up, to take the path that leads to spiritual maturity.

We should know that this means, not only that there is

no magic guidance but that genuine ideals are unavailing, too, unless they are fully related to realities. This requires not only devotion but intelligence. We are supposed to "love the Lord, our God" not only with our hearts but with our minds. This cannot mean that we should love him with lazy minds, dull with a perpetual torpor. We must love him with minds that we use—and use continuously and diligently.

The truth is that the childhood of the race is over. There is no room left anywhere for spiritual immaturity. What we need now is a grown-up idealism, mature in concept and no less mature in application. Only so can we solve our world-wide problems: problems that are no longer remote but have come to us at last right on our own doorsteps. Only so can we rebuild the fabric of our common life together, embodying ideals of fairness, kindness, sympathy and love. For in some parts of the earth, these qualities have almost vanished, driven before the elemental fury of war and withered by its aftermath, reducing mankind to the level of the hungry brute. They will only return if, besides believing in them and invoking them, we decide to embody them and provide a world in which they can live.

The way before us is the hard way, the way of grown-up people in a grown-up world. The way of taking responsibility, of sifting truth from error, of separating the difficult right from the plausible wrong. The way of praying, not that God shall take away our burdens but that God shall so dwell in our thoughts and rule our lives that we shall become strong enough to carry these burdens—to carry them until our strength is such that they are burdens no longer and we bear them buoyantly and lightly.

If we try to run away from this new moral growth that is demanded of us, this new and larger application of religion, this spiritual maturity that leaves the childhood of the race behind, the penalty will be sure and punctual. For we are facing a demand that is no longer a prediction: its time has come. The religious applications that seemed enough in the past are no longer enough. We must press on to new aims and larger purposes—none of which will be easy nor even the formulation of them quick or simple to achieve. But nonetheless, we need not do these things out of spiritual emptiness. We need not do them out of overstrain and doubt. We can have this faith: that what the life of the world outside us demands, the life of the spirit within us can supply—whenever we are willing that it shall.

16

Neither Optimist Nor Pessimist

FEW SUBJECTS have been more discussed than the comparative merits of optimism and pessimism, but not much of the discussion has been useful. To the optimist, pessimism is a sort of cowardice and he denounces it as treason to the human venture. Despondent people have become so through weakness of character, he says, and looks upon their gloomy views as a sign of moral deficiency. "Why can't they be hopeful like everyone else?" he asks. "Why do they need to depress other people by making the worst of things? What good ever came from looking at the darker side?" And he implies that pessimism is a deliberate perversity. A virtuous man, he insists, is always hopeful; he is not himself discouraged and he dislikes to discourage other people. To an optimist, therefore, optimism is on the side of goodness and pessimism is allied with evil.

To the pessimist, however, all this is so much chatter. He does not deny that he may be morally deficient but he believes that everyone else is, too. Defects of character, he says, will be found in pessimists and optimists alike, but he thinks that optimists have an additional deficiency: weakness of mind. How else could they be optimists? They look at life, not as it is but through a veil of wishful thinking. Their buoyancy is due to animal spirits. They are unperceptive; they do not see the facts. For all of which reasons they are doubtless to be pitied—but also, so far as possible, avoided.

To a pessimist, an optimist is irritating. He sounds childish. His cheerful prattle is merely further proof that humanity is hopeless. Indeed, it has been said that a pessimist is a man who has spent too much time in the company of optimists.

As we listen to these discussions, we wonder if there is any value in them. Might it not be that optimism and pessimism are merely temperamental opposites? So that some people, for certain unfathomable reasons, are sanguine and hopeful while others are despondent and morose? Both, in a sense, enjoy themselves. Optimists are happy in their hopefulness; pessimists are pleased that they are not optimists. Perhaps it is inexplicable. Possibly the whole matter is summed up in the saying that an optimist sees a bottle as half full whereas a pessimist sees it as half empty. What the bottle is supposed to contain I do not know, but if it is consumable I suspect that its contents would have no other effect than to fortify the optimist in his optimism and confirm the pessimist in his gloom.

Here, however, we are thinking in extremes. It has been said that a pessimist is one who, when he has the choice of two evils, chooses both. But not all pessimism goes that far. Nor even as far as the pessimism described by Bernard Shaw, who said that a pessimist is one who thinks everybody else "as nasty as himself, and hates them for it." On the other hand, not all optimists are as badly off as those portrayed by Elbert Hubbard. An optimist, he wrote, is "a neurotic person with gooseflesh and teeth a-chatter, trying hard to be brave." Optimism is not necessarily just "whistling to keep your courage up." It can have as good a rational ground as pessimism, and at times be genuinely braver.

I remember some years ago hearing a speaker—a distinguished historian—dismiss optimism as invariably stupid. To illustrate his point he told the story of two young Irishmen in a Canadian regiment in the First World War. They were going into the trenches with the odds stacked against them, and their Captain, feeling rather desperate, had promised that for every enemy soldier killed he would pay ten dollars. "They're coming!" said one of the Irishmen. "Who's coming?" asked the other. "The enemy," replied the first one, "and they're ten-thousand strong." "Ten-thousand strong!" exclaimed his buddy. "Let's get shooting! Our fortune's made!" And the speaker went on to declare that those who see opportunity in the threat of calamity are just as dim-witted as the Irishman.

But in voicing that opinion he was not a good historian. Calamities are certainly not to be taken lightly; nevertheless, they *have* been seized as opportunities. The calamity of the fall of the Roman Empire—and most historians agree, I think, that it *was* a calamity—became to the early Christians a very definite opportunity, and they took it and established Christendom. This did not make the calamity unreal; to those who were engulfed by it, it was an unrelieved disaster. It may have been disastrous to some of the Christians; yet there is no denying that to the Christian movement generally, it was an opportunity. Whether they were optimists, of course, is not a simple question. In a certain sense, they had given up the present world and had set their hopes upon the next, which from this world's viewpoint is pessimistic; nevertheless, they had a positive belief in their own mission and it was strong enough to bring them to victory.

In our own situation, what we must come to, I think, is something better than a choice between optimism and pessimism—which in actual fact is what the early Christians did. To look only on the bright side is neither wise nor virtuous. It cannot be wise because it obscures the fact that the dark side is just as real as the bright and that we have to contend with it. It is not virtuous because nothing is virtuous that blinds itself to facts. What is there that is morally good about saying that there *is* no dark side, or that if there is we ought not to look at it? If we don't look at it we shall not be able to deal with it; and deal with it we must or be defeated.

The attitude of some optimists—I think other optimists would call them shallow ones—is like that of the London cockney who was found by a policeman searching in the gutter beneath the light of a street lamp. "What did you lose?" asked the policeman. "A shilling," the man replied. "Where did you lose it?" the policeman inquired after helping vainly for a few moments in the search. "Fifty yards down the street," the man reluctantly admitted, "but the light's better here."

Unfortunately, there are people who rejoice in their optimism who are no more intelligent than the man in this story. Instead of looking where they need to look if their efforts are to be successful, they prefer the areas that are more brightly lighted. "Yes, indeed," they say, when the dark places are pointed out to them, "but let's not look in that direction; let's look over here where the light is brighter."

There is not much to be gained from that sort of optimism; and there is no virtue in it. Far from being morally superior, it is distinctly escapist and should be condemned. It is also, of course, an inheritance from a happier world. In the nineteenth century, it seemed natural to many (though not by any means to all) to look always on the bright side. This was true of many who spoke for religion in that period, and some of them carried it to embarrassing extremes. Indeed, I am sorry to say that one of my own predecessors (in my pulpit in Washington), Dr. Edward Everett Hale, was addicted at times to this overemphasis. In the year 1870 (of all years!), in words that became famous, he advised us

> To look up and not down
> To look forward and not back,
> To look out and not in, and
> To lend a hand.

I hope I shall not seem lacking in reverence for his memory if I say that the only part of this saying that is good religion is the advice "to lend a hand."

If we look up and not down we shall blind ourselves to the evils that are all about us, and sooner or later stumble headlong into trouble that we might have avoided. If we had been intended to look up and not down, our necks would have been framed accordingly—and, as a matter of fact, there is always a danger of rearranging them that way: a danger, I mean, that those who look up and not down will get stiff-necked, holding their heads up with a sort of muscle-bound piety. We should look down just as religiously as we look up, seeing the dirt as clearly as we do the sky. Jesus did; and so did every other great religious teacher.

As for looking forward and not back, this would mean throwing away all the lessons of history. The neglect of those lessons has been one of the greatest curses of modern life and has caused us to fall into errors that familiarity with the past would have warned us to avoid.

Furthermore, to believe that the world began when *we* did—that for all intents and purposes our own age is the only one that counts—is not only ignorant but arrogant. To look back as well as forward is to give ourselves a lesson in humility.

When it comes to looking out and not in, the psychologists will tell us—and they are right—that unless we look into our own lives for long enough to discover what is really so about us, we are hell-bent for trouble. In this they would be backed by all the wisdom of the ages. Far too many people have allowed their religion to become shallow, and thus in spite of the good causes they have served while "looking out and not in," their understanding of moral and spiritual law has been extremely feeble. Instead, for instance, of facing tragedy—which is a real part of human life—they have looked away from it and have done the same with other things they did not wish to face. This kind of optimism is not religious at all; it is irreligious—as all things are that run for refuge to the false and the delusive.

Not that Edward Everett Hale intended such results; far from it. But speaking when he did, and with the emphasis of his particular time, he over-stated his case. Great men do that as well as lesser ones. And all men, of course, are molded—some more, some less—by the time in which they live. Optimism seemed natural (to the comfortable part of the world) in the nineteenth century. One is reminded of the centenarian who was asked by a newspaper man the inevitable question: to what did he attribute his long life? "I attribute it," he replied, "to the fact that it was my good fortune to be born a century ago." Well, if the question had been asked a little differently and had concerned itself with happiness rather than longevity, he might have said that he attributed his happiness, his sense of security, or his optimism, if he had them, to having been born when these things were part of a widespread expectation—which they were a century ago.

Today we know—or should—that an unthinking cheerfulness, a blind belief that good is inevitable, is a handicap not a help. It separates us from reality. And if it does that, it also weakens our religion. For it is reality that religion must face—must face and must contend with—and if it is too weak to do it, defeat is certain.

On the other hand, there is no superiority in pessimism. If the optimist is an escapist at one extreme, the pessimist is equally so at another. He says that nothing is worth doing, and so he *does* nothing. This is cowardice. It is also irrational. For the evidence is just as much against the pessimist as the optimist. Things *have* been done—and done because there were people who worked for what they hoped for. It is not true that humanity has won no victories. Yet such victories are only possible when people believe in them. If they give up before they start, they don't start. Nor is it true that pessimists are necessarily of stronger mind than optimists. What they think of as intellectual superiority is very often just emotional sensitivity. They are afraid of the task before them, afraid of the effort exacted, afraid of the chance of failure. They do not want to try. They are pessimists because they are not morally tough enough to be anything else.

This is as great a peril as exaggerated optimism. At the present time, optimism is receding, and probably rather fast. In recoil from previous far-too-hopeful expectations, which they now see to have been delusive, an increasing multitude of moderns are becoming pessimistic. This manifests itself as a feeling of helplessness, a belief that nothing can be done by effort or resolve: that whatever happens must be counted quite inevitable and that it will come by the working of fate or fortune. Neither the will of God nor the will of man enters into their calculations.

This, as we would know if we had looked back as well as forward, has happened before in history, and not once but many times. The episode of which we have most knowledge, however, was the one described by Sir Gilbert Murray as the "failure of nerve" in the Greco-Roman world: the "failure of nerve" which began in the fourth century B.C. and continued until the establishment of Christianity. What happened, according to Professor Murray, was in the first place a sort of exhaustion of the spirit of freedom, including free choice concerning the future. Confident inquiry gave way to anguished uncertainty. The most to be hoped for was fortitude in confronting fate and necessity. As the Roman historian, Pliny, records it, "Throughout the whole world at every hour and place, by every voice Fortune alone is invoked and her name is spoken; she is the one defendant, the one culprit, the one cause. . . . We are so much at the mercy of chance that chance is our God."

That is what happened at an earlier time when optimism became exhausted, and that is what is threatening us, now. The only escape from pessimism at that earlier time was a stoical dependence upon fortune, a residual wish that chance or fate would turn aside the logic of events and bring about a happy ending.

Meanwhile, of course, the people themselves held within their own hands the means to mold their destiny. As we do, too. But it involved deliberate aim and purpose; and it involved exertion. Which is exactly our own situation. Everything that happened in that earlier time was *allowed* to happen—*by people who could have made things happen differently.*

It is this that we need to see. Neither optimism nor pessimism as commonly defined has any power to help us. But *affirmation* can help us. When we affirm our aim, when we say that "this is what *should* happen" and follow it with "this is what we shall *make* to happen," we have taken the path that holds the promise of victory. It may be a painful path. Nothing whatever could make it easy. But we can set our feet in it and begin to travel it, when we have so resolved.

In this event we are neither optimists nor pessimists, but what I would call *affirmatists.* We are not optimists because we do not hold that events are sure to favor us; and we are not pessimists because we do not believe that we are foredoomed to be defeated; what we affirm is that events can be influenced, that we can largely control them, that good is possible if we ourselves decide upon it. And thus, as I say, we are not optimists, contributing by our escapism to the deficiencies that issue in disaster; nor are we pessimists, releasing ourselves from our obligations on the false ground that failure is inescapable. We are affirmatists: irrespective of circumstances, which may at any time be either favorable or unfavorable, encouraging or forbidding, we devote ourselves to what is needed to avert disaster and turn it into victory.

As already indicated, the victory of Christianity in the days of the crumbling Roman Empire was largely due to its affirmatism. It was not optimistic; it was not pessimistic. It affirmed a faith, a purpose, a duty. And thus in a negative world, it was positive, affirmative. It called upon people to *do* something—to do what was right. It asked them to live differently—not as children of fate but as

children of God. It awakened their will power and invoked
their capacity to love. A world falling apart could be
drawn together again—by faith, hope and love. Those are
the words. Not that the early Church lived up to them—
not by a long way. Yet, so great is the power of these
three—of faith, hope and love—that even though the
Church fell short of the possibilities—grievously short—
what was done was nevertheless potent enough to turn
calamity into opportunity and build a new civilization
upon the ruins of the old.

Affirmation is faith: the faith that good is possible and
that it can overcome evil; affirmation is hope: the reasonable hope that man can bring to pass the ends he works
for; affirmation is love: the love of the good that unfetters
the soul and expels the power of evil. It is not optimism,
and not pessimism, but affirmation that is true religion.

If religion were optimism, we should never have heard
of a Jesus agonizing in the Garden of Gethsemane; if it
were pessimism, Jesus would never have begun his mission: there would have been no basis for it. What we read
is that Jesus went on with his work both under sunny
skies in Galilee and in the grimness of the journey to
Jerusalem. For religion is affirmation.

17

What to Do with Gloom

IN ONE OF the creation myths, it is related of Prometheus, who is supposed to have brought life as well as fire to the earth, that in the process of molding the animals out of clay he used up all the available supply of water. Consequently, when he came to make man there was nothing with which to bind the clay together and he found it breaking apart and crumbling in his hands.

Some of the gods suggested that this was an omen that man had better be left uncreated. Why not be satisfied with the multitude of living creatures already in existence? But Prometheus refused to be frustrated. He looked up into the sky for signs of rain: there was not a cloud to be seen beneath the brazen vault of heaven. He searched the Garden of Creation for undiscovered wells and springs: the gods had dried them all up. Even the grass was beginning to be parched.

At last, Prometheus threw himself down on the ground and wept, and then, while his grief was still unspent, he saw that his tears had moistened the clay and that it held together. Swiftly, he molded it afresh, and before the sun went down was ready to breathe the breath of his own life into the image he had fashioned; and man, the child of desire and sorrow, was created.

What the myth means, of course, is obvious. Yet, until very recently it was a meaning that a large part of the modern world had forgotten. Sadness was regarded as something alien to normal life, a mood that was unavoidable, perhaps, in misfortune, and almost inevitable in bereavement, but a sort of malady of the emotions to be banished as quickly as possible. Brightness and optimism were called for in all circumstances; more and more opportunities were being afforded for gaiety; newer and newer ways were being invented for cheering ourselves up. And, in fact, everything was so good, or going to be so good, that there was really no excuse for gloom.

When such a brilliant publicist as William Ralph Inge, Dean of St. Paul's in London, insisted upon taking a graver view of human affairs, the newspapers dubbed him "the Gloomy Dean." His notoriety was considerable, his popularity rather low. No one wanted to listen to what the Gloomy Dean was really saying, namely, that optimism is too shallow a faith, that it does not fit the facts—not all of them—and that if the modern age is to save itself from the same fate that has overtaken previous very confident ages, it must reckon with realities from which, in shallowness and petulance, it turns aside and looks the other way.

But the Gloomy Dean was only reinforcing what the Promethean myth had tried to tell us long before: that in the composition of human life, tears are just as natural as laughter; that the substance of sorrow has been in us from the beginning; that you cannot have desire without heartache, or feel the poignancy of yearning without knowing the closeness of despair. What the myth tells us is that this was always so. Or, as Swinburne re-tells it in his *Atalanta in Calydon,*

> Before the beginning of years,
>   There came to the making of man,
> Time, with a gift of tears;

> Grief, with a glass that ran;
> Pleasure, with pain for leaven;
> Summer, with flowers that fell;
> Remembrance fallen from heaven;
> And madness risen from hell;
> Strength without hands to smite;
> Love that endures for a breath;
> Night, the shadow of light,
> And life, the shadow of death.

If this, then, is the nature of man, of what use is it to say of gloom, as some do, that the thing to do is avoid it? How can you avoid the inevitable? Or pretend to make no room for what springs from the essential nature of your own life? Such advice is too facile, too unperceiving; sometimes, it is nothing but mockery.

It is true, of course, that cheerfulness comes more readily to some people than to others. It may be true, as we are occasionally told, that there are those who escape despondency almost altogether. But whether this is entirely fortunate is quite a question! For my own part, I leave it as a question that I do not presume to answer. I merely mention in passing that very little of importance in the world has been accomplished by people who are consistently cheerful.

I am not speaking of outward appearances, which are often deceptive, but of inner realities. Indeed, it is quite doubtful whether consistent cheerfulness is truly compatible with the full use of the mental faculties. I remember that Pearl Buck, in one of her books, portrays a little Chinese girl with an undeveloped mind, and the mother of the little girl, whenever she needs to explain to a stranger that her daughter is not normal, simply says, "All her thoughts are happy ones." We have to recognize, I think, that if acute melancholia can be diagnosed as psychopathic, so can perpetual hilarity.

Even when it is some distance from needing institutional treatment, perpetual hilarity can be disturbing; it can also be extremely irritating. The person who finds everything just wonderful and "smiles and whistles under all circumstances" may be quite exhilarating for half an hour or so, but if it lasts much longer his victims clench their hands behind their back and wonder whether they can get away before giving in to an overwhelming impulse to choke him.

Even when such cheerfulness excites no wrath, it can be repugnant to a normal person. The reason is, of course, that something common-sensical within us demands a proper reckoning with realities. We are repelled by the superficiality of this sort of cheerfulness. We want to go away somewhere and feel as gloomy as possible—just to recover our mental balance.

And in the present world, where there is so much of misery spread out over the face of the earth, and so much of foreboding as we look towards the future, even if gloom were not already a natural mood of human life, coming and going as all moods come and go, it would seem necessary to invite it, at any rate for long enough to let us feel the full force of the circumstances by which we are surrounded. For surely we should be lacking in emotional depth if we could really understand our situation and never feel depressed.

Let us admit, then, and freely, that the notion of getting rid of gloom by reciting to ourselves a few well chosen "pollyannaisms" is both futile and absurd. Let us go on to admit that if it could succeed—which it cannot under present conditions—such a shallow success would be unwholesome and unworthy. Let us even go a little deeper and acknowledge that sadness is a natural part of life: that a mature man or woman accepts it. It is not only that personal disappointment or bereavement can cause sadness: the contemplation of the world itself—the world man makes and breaks—should cause it.

In all that life is, even in its joys, there is at least the hint of sadness. Always we hear what Wordsworth called "the still, sad music of humanity."

> I have learned, [he says]
> To look on nature, not as in the hour
> Of thoughtless youth; but hearing oftentimes
> The still, sad music of humanity . . .

But he does not find it merely painful. He has discovered, he goes on to tell us, that what at first was dejection and despondency can deepen into something that carries within it the pulse and power of life itself, something that brings to the soul its own revelation of the meaning hidden within the mystery. For, he continues,

> I have felt
> A presence that disturbs me with the joy
> Of elevated thoughts; a sense sublime
> Of something far more deeply interfused,
> Whose dwelling is the light of setting suns,
> And the round ocean and the living air,
> And the blue sky, and in the mind of man.

And since Wordsworth is by no means alone in this discovery, we can be sure that despondency and gloom, and indeed sadness in any of its intensities, can make us far more sensitive to ultimate meanings, can deepen us spiritually, can bring us closer to the greatness which is always trying to lay its touch upon us—or, in shorter, more familiar words, can help us to grow a soul.

That, it seems to me, is the first thing to know about gloom: that it is not necessarily a misfortune or a deprivation. If you can learn how to treat it, how to live with it when it visits you, it can be a means of spiritual development. This will never be so if you try to treat it superficially, or if you take fright at tragic realities. It will never be so if you attempt to bolster up your life with artificial gaieties. You have to accept sadness—yet, you must never surrender to it.

That is the second thing. You must never surrender to sadness. There are people who turn it into a permanent melancholy, so that it becomes an emotional indulgence—something quite demoralizing. Because they find themselves sometimes pessimistic, they insist upon being always pessimistic. Thus they are able to sever themselves from what needs to be done in the world. "It is all hopeless," they say, "quite hopeless!" And because they can say it is hopeless, they feel excused from trying to *do* anything about it. This is surrender. Just as "pollyannaism" can be one form of escape—a shallow one—so pessimism can be another—also shallow. Let us analyze it.

The pessimist convinces himself that because he has succumbed to melancholy, he is somehow a superior sort of person. He has faced the worst, he says, and is not deceived like other people. But he *is* deceived. He deceives *himself*. He has *not* faced the worst. He has only glanced at it—and run away in complete retreat. He has given up. If he had faced the worst and kept on facing it, he would have found it necessary to *do* something. Even in his thinking he would have gone on with the struggle until he found convictions: the conviction, for instance, that whatever happens, life is full of its own great purpose, a purpose that *must* be served; and that this is a reality woven into the texture of all other realities. Gloom can never be a real excuse for moral cowardice. Despondency never disables anybody without his own consent—his own decision that it shall. On the contrary, it can improve his understanding of what is necessary and make him much surer in all that he undertakes. It can increase his moral energy. It can give him clearer comprehension of other people. It can show a man how to fight without malice, and win without boasting, and lose without bitterness. It can do these things because his own spirit has been deepened—if he so wills it.

But let us try to find the simplest, clearest possible way of saying all this: let us make it very practical. There are many people who feel gloomy today who have never made friends with sadness in the past and so are quite at a loss to know how to get along with it. They are accustomed to live and work only from feelings of optimism. How can we state the matter so that all will understand?

Fortunately, we *can* state it. We can state it in a single sentence. *When you feel gloomy, put your gloom to work!* Let me explain just why it is that this is practical advice. Gloom is an emotional state, just as mirth is an emotional state, or joyousness. And emotion is a form of energy. Indeed, at the human level, emotion is the one form that energy takes. And energy can be put to work. Almost any kind of energy.

What energy do you suppose it is that gives to poets their power of expression? It can be joy, of course. Many a sonnet is an outpouring of rapture. But it can also be grief. Or just a bleak and deadly melancholy. Some of the greatest poetry that has ever been written has come from gloom; and not necessarily gloomy poetry, either. Emotional energy, like other forms of energy, is convertible.

This is so at every level. The work done need not have the color of the emotional energy that produced it. Gloom can produce other things than pathos. It was Aristotle, I think, who said that "melancholy men of all others are the most witty." There is no doubt, I think, that the whole field of literature would corroborate his opinion. Yet, the wit is not all satire. There is nothing about gloom that makes it inevitably corrosive. Any emotional intensification can liberate energies of every sort—including the most wholesome.

If it is true that musicians, for instance, have often been morose—and I think it *is* true—we have to admit, nonetheless, that their music is not imprisoned by their moods. Even melancholy music can raise itself beyond the level of mere gloom. It is true, of course, that such a piece as Tschaikowsky's *Symphonie Pathétique* luxuriates in sorrow, and is, to that extent, emotional indulgence. But it need not have been so. Music need not stop at registering a mood; it can use the mood to press beyond it—often into ultimate mysteries of experience that are not translatable from music into any other medium.

It often seems to me, when I listen to a symphony, that the composer begins with something out of the struggle of his own experience, perhaps out of his own defeat, and in the weeks and months of composing, gradually transforms what he began with into something universal and victorious. I am aware that to some extent this can be a technical accomplishment, once you have mastered the trick; but I am also aware that no amount of technical skill can achieve alone what it takes emotional force to accomplish; and inasmuch as no one can read the biographies of the great composers without knowing how fearfully some of them were afflicted with melancholy, and sometimes not of a very lofty order, it seems to me certain that what they did was to employ their emotional energy —no matter what form it took—to create their music.

So that I say again, when you are afflicted with gloom, put it to work. If you do not happen to be a poet or a musician (and it is not in the least necessary that you should be), put your gloom to work in what you *can* do. Remember that "only the duties of the heart can truly console the heart." Don't luxuriate in gloom; don't make of it an emotional indulgence; and don't think you have to wait until something happens to make you feel more cheerful. Particularly, do not make the mistake of trying to cheer yourself up with something trivially optimistic. That only leads to exasperation.

When I feel gloomy, myself, I always pick out the most despondent poetry I know, or the most melancholy music, and the specific gravity of my own gloom is so much lighter than this dense melancholy in which I immerse it that after a while it always bobs up and floats upon it! So that I feel comparatively buoyant. At any rate, I am then ready to do some work. And if personal testimony counts for anything, I am willing to admit that some of my most cheerful sermons have been written out of moods of frustration or depression. There is no difficulty about it at all. You simply give your mind to the work.

I am sure that this is possible in almost any pursuit. And you will never end up merely gloomy. There may be a remaining element of sadness in your mood—of one intensity or another—but there will also be courage in it, and something that smiles—smiles back at you—and at last, paradoxically, no small amount of buoyancy. The most secure gaiety in the world, perhaps the only gaiety that is really secure, is distilled from sadness.

Nor do I mean by this that the gaiety is qualified or forced. Quite the contrary. Only those who understand tragedy really appreciate comedy. If you find that too paradoxical, may I recommend you to visit the Lincoln Memorial some time and take a long look at the face of the greatest of all Americans. If you know his story, you know that he was the most melancholy of men—at one time so much the prisoner of gloom that his warmest friends wondered if he could ever be delivered from it. He never lost his melancholy. The sadness of all human life, like the sadness of his own great, tragic destiny, is deeply engraved in the lines of his face. It is for that most of all, without quite understanding it, that Americans love him—and love him best. There is no more tragic figure than Abraham Lincoln. But was there ever an American with a keener sense of comedy? Or one who knew more than he how to put gloom to work?

What else was it that he did? As John Dyer, an eighteenth century poet once wrote,

> There is a kindly mood of melancholy
>   That wings the soul.

That's it! Carrying melancholy from bitterness to kindliness, and giving the power of flight to spirit and imagination. It is thus that vision grows, and with it, resolve. Out of it come gentleness, comprehension, tenderness—and yet unyielding firmness.

This can happen to anybody who will put his gloom to work, who will let despondency stretch his heart—until it is large enough for love. It can happen to anybody who will give himself, and go on giving and keep on giving, until he turns despair to hope, and desolation to faith, and emptiness into the temple of the living God.

Perhaps that is what God is doing to us in this generation—at no matter what cost: we who have achieved so much, who have known so many triumphs and such dark defeats; we who have filled the world to overflowing with man-made miseries, and meanwhile have pretended that only happiness is tenable, that only happiness is real. Perhaps our time has come to reckon with forlornness, to face desperation, to know the meaning of deprivation.

We must be deepened. Until we are, we are not good enough. We cannot do what is commanded of us. New buoyancies will come—some day. New confidence, and new assurance. But we of this bleakest moment and this darkened hour—we must save a world even though to save it we must lose it. We must hear as we have never heard before, those words of Jesus about losing a world to gain a soul.

Shall we fear it? Surrendering to despondency because so much is called for, so much demanded, from those who are not yet worthy? Or shall we not rather take all the emotional intensities of every kind—even gloom—and make them work for God and the morning of a better world?

18

How Much Can Human Nature
Be Changed?

WHENEVER THE magnitude of modern problems is discussed, the question is raised as to whether human nature is equal to such large requirements. The burden is not a light one; will our capacity be overtaxed? As a building contractor expressed it, after listening silently to an argument on this subject, "How far can you carry a ton-and-a-half in a half-ton truck?" It is a question that needs to be answered. Upon the basis of past performance, how may we rate our capacity? What reason do we have for thinking we can solve the problems that the modern age has thrust upon us?

Does history make us confident that we can avoid wars, or arrest the decline of a civilization, or achieve the necessary transitions in world society without calamity? Do we see in previous experience a basis for supposing that we shall act wisely rather than foolishly, promptly rather than tardily, vigorously rather than sluggishly, in matters of decisive importance?

Apparently, the answer to all these questions is far from reassuring. While from time to time human nature has been equal to the strains imposed upon it, it has frequently broken down when the load grew really heavy. Unless, therefore, we can do better in the future than we have in the past, our situation is a grim one.

This, however, raises a second point. If human nature has proved inadequate on previous occasions, is this because of inherent incapacity or can something be done about it? To what extent—if any—can human nature be changed? And here we come to the really crucial question. If we do no better in the future than was done in the past, our prospect is not a bright one. But in order to do better we shall have to reach a higher level. About that there seems to be no doubt. Our belief, therefore, in the power of human nature to surmount our present difficulties depends upon our confidence that human nature can be improved. But can it?

There are those, apparently, who think it can. If they thought otherwise, they would not exhort us, as Dr. Overstreet does, and Dr. Brock Chisholm of the United Nations, to have mature minds, or tell us how clearly we must begin to think and how responsibly we need to act. For they know that these things are not customary with us. Most of the time, our minds are not mature, and we neither think rationally nor act responsibly. What they depend upon, then, these who exhort us, is not only that human nature can be changed for the better, but that this can happen quite suddenly and drastically. But can it?

There are those who say it is impossible. Human nature is what it always was, they tell us, and its characteristics are unalterable. Why should we suppose that people will be different today than they were a hundred years ago, or a thousand years ago? Why should they be any better in the future than the past? Only the externals change, the customs and the fashions; the essentials all remain the same.

Some of those who take this view are admittedly not thoughtful. They have not so much formed an opinion as received an impression. Emotionally, they welcome this impression. If nothing is possible, nothing need be attempted, and this, of course, saves a lot of trouble. In their hearts, these people do not *want* human nature to be changed. They want to remain undisturbed at the level of life they are now living. To the question now before us they make no useful contribution.

But among those who think that human nature cannot be changed—or at least not very much—there are others whom no one could call thoughtless. They appeal to the great thinkers of the ages; to Aristotle, for instance, whom it would be very difficult to relegate to such a category. Aristotle had thought a good deal about the possibilities of human progress and came to the conclusion that they scarcely existed. Even slavery, he said, would never be abolished; it is rooted in aboriginal human nature. Some men, he contended, have it in their nature to be slaves, others to be masters. There will always be men of the one sort and also of the other, and therefore slavery will be perpetual.

Nor should we suppose that if Aristotle were with us today, and obliged to hear himself quoted, he would feel embarrassed. "My prediction was substantially right," he would say; "the form of slavery changes, but not the fact. There are still those with power and those who are powerless. But instead of manacles you have manipulation. I know all about democracy," he would continue; "we had it in Athens. And nevertheless, the master-minded ruled it over the slave-minded, just as they do with you. Moreover, Athenian democracy did not last. Nor did Roman. Nor did modern democracy in Italy or Germany; nor has the promise of it been fulfilled in Russia or in China. And yours will not last. There are those who have it in their

natures to be masters," he would repeat, "and those who
are fitted only to be slaves."

Many historians would agree with Aristotle; and no
small number of philosophers. They confirm that nothing
changes but the form. Essentially, whatever happens has
already happened before. Civilizations, Spengler informs
us, follow the same general pattern: they emerge, they
grow, they flourish, they decline, they die; and at each
stage they do substantially what earlier civilizations have
done. And he offers us impressive data to confirm it. So
do other historians. They insist that history repeats itself,
and that it always must, because human nature remains
the same.

Where, then, do we stand? The weight of opinion seems
to be against us. Most of those who have investigated the
subject are pessimistic. No matter what the need for a
higher level, they are afraid that we shall not arrive at it.
Must we accept this position? Does reason require it of
us? Are we without alternatives? Is there no hope?

I believe the contrary. Historians have not pronounced
our doom. What they indicate is not that all our efforts
will be futile, but that the measure of them must be great.
Human nature is not *easily* changed; no, but it *can* be
changed. It *can* be changed for the simple reason that it
has been changed. It was through change that it became
what it now is, and there is no reason for supposing that
the process is completed.

Even the most obdurate pessimist must admit that there
was once a time when human nature was less than it now
is. Indeed, there was a period when there *was* no human
nature. Unless the theory of the evolution of species is
erroneous, we are derived from lower forms of life. This
would not have been possible without change. Our pro-

genitors had to move from one level to another, either gradually and continuously, as some believe, or through more violent transitions, as is believed by others. As a result, there came at length to be the creature known as man.

He was not the same, however, at his first emergence— if we can speak of a first emergence—as he was a little later. Even physically he kept changing. His posture became more upright, his hands less clumsy. Above all, his brain developed. There was an immense difference between the earliest men and the men of the Stone Age. And at least an equal difference between men of the Stone Age and those of the era covered by history.

Nor must we think of man as merely individual. His development has also been social. The scope of change between ancient societies wandering in the desert and the advanced society represented by a modern nation is enormous. To say that man is the same socially in a tribal unit as he is in a country ruled under the United States Constitution is palpable absurdity. There is no question whatever about the *fact* that human nature changes. And in spite of the cynics, there is no serious question of the changes being improvements. I have not noticed any cynics whose revulsion against modern society drives them running to an aboriginal tribe for refuge. A cynic, apparently, likes to live where he can eat regularly without having to hunt or grow his own food; he wants to live where he is protected by law rather than by primitive custom, where there is medical care and a good hospital; and generally, he wants friends and interesting conversation, books to read, music perhaps, satirical magazines, newspapers to provide him with his daily food for scorn, and all the privileges of a highly developed culture.

Although he would rather die than admit it, he probably wants to live in a society that cares about moral values: where truth is respected even if sometimes betrayed, and in which there is a general esteem for justice. He even needs—though this may be the one thing above all others that he will not admit—a society influenced by religion: not primitive religion but ethical religion, brought about by change in human nature, a society that has felt the influence of exemplars and prophets, sages, saints and martyrs.

What sense is there, then, in saying that human nature is the same thing that it was when it was born in the jungle? Human nature *has* changed: it has *improved*. And it can go a lot further in the same direction.

But here we come to something else. It is contended that all these changes may very well have been gradual. Ours, however, is not a situation where the gradual can save us. How *fast* can human nature change?

Scientifically, this is not a question to which there is a ready answer. The Marxists were being scientific—so they thought—when they asserted that human nature could be transformed through the communist revolution. Change the conditions—the environment—and instantly you change the man. So they said. But their changes have proved for the worse. The atavistic in human nature came to the top; and evil, not good, seized control of their experiment. This will remain so, apparently, not only for a brief, disruptive period of transition but for as long as the communist experiment endures. For a dictatorship to change us for the better, it must be a dictatorship of men so wise, so benevolent, so sincere, so unselfish, so altogether virtuous, that if we could find such men, and in sufficient numbers for the purpose, there would be no need for a dictatorship.

Human nature would be changing rapidly enough without one.

As perhaps it will. Not by the communist method but in resistance to that method, through a combination of intention and necessity. Let us go back once more to what the past can teach us. When primitive men were faced with new necessities they either rose to the challenge or perished. If, for instance, an earthquake destroyed a cave and no other cave was available, the survivors either evolved another form of shelter or perished. If one area became uninhabitable, primitive man moved to another. In this new area, conditions would be different and he would have to find new skills to make him equal to them. Quite evidently, he managed to do these things. Otherwise, instead of being our ancestor, his species would have disappeared. Clearly, then, when change is urgent the power to change accelerates, called forth by the relentless challenge of necessity.

Toynbee tells us that this is the key to history. Necessity is the *stimulus;* progress is the *response:* from this has come the entire story of civilized advance. He would add, I think, that besides necessity there must be opportunity. A people driven from their territory by invaders develop a new and perhaps better territory; a tribe subject to pillage builds a walled city at a defensible point along a river, and thus raises the level of its life; to survive and grow, maritime commerce is established by people who live on islands. The illustrations are innumerable. But what they come down to, apparently, is that human nature can change, gradually *or* rapidly, when conditions require it and opportunities exist.

And thus we come to our own situation. The necessity is very urgent. If we are to manage the modern world in such a way that it will not destroy itself, we must achieve the capacity for it. This is our necessity, as great as any that has ever been faced in the past.

With it comes our opportunity. The possibility of a good world, both materially and spiritually, is entirely real. We have the skill for it—the technical skill—as no generation ever had it before us. Our science, intelligently managed, could free the world not only from disease and famine but from almost all its evils and afflictions, so far as these are rooted in material needs. Our opportunity is as real as our necessity.

What, then, of our capacity? As we have seen, human nature is adaptable. We have the possibility of change. The only question is our will to make it actual. Mentality is not lacking. If it were, how could we have accomplished what we have with science? It is *morally* that we are too much chained to the past! Yet we can change our moral attitude *just by changing it*. As we have seen earlier in this book, one of the saddest and most foolish superstitions of the modern world is that people can arrive at righteousness without will-power, that we can build good characters (we prefer the word *personality* to *character*, of course) without effort. None of this is true.

If we are to change, it will have to be by resolving upon it, by making an act of will. Just as we learn to swim by swimming: that is to say, by getting into the water, propelling ourselves by suitable movements, learning to breathe properly—and all the rest. But you will never swim just by thinking about the water, or by trying to devise a way of swimming without getting wet. It is the same with almost everything which at one time we are not able to do and then attain the skill for. You learn to play the piano by mastering the notation and practicing on the keyboard; you learn to speak in public by standing before an audience and attempting to say what you intend to say; you learn to saw the end of a board square by taking up a saw, holding it properly and sawing down the scribed line until you can do it well.

Too many people think—or perhaps I should say hope —that there is some way of arriving at what they want without effort, particularly without effort of the will. I even remember a young man who once came to see me to ask how he could discover whether the lady of his choice would marry him. I said, "Ask her." "But she might say 'No,'" he replied. "In that case," I said, "you will have your answer." "Well," he went on, "when I'm with her, I feel nervous and no matter what I do, the words come out all wrong." "Don't worry," I said, "even the wrong words will give her the right idea, and if she wants you she'll marry you anyway." Which she did.

This, however, was partly a case of timidity. The greater obstacle is indolence, a self-indulgent moral softness. It hopes for a miracle—the maximum result with minimum effort.

I repeat, therefore, that an act of will—indeed, many acts of will—are indispensable. But we *can* change human nature, and in sufficient measure for the purpose, if we resolve upon it. That, as I understand it, is basic to the message of religion. When Jesus said, "Repent," he meant not only that people should feel sorry that they had done badly but that they should begin to do better, and live on a new and higher level of life. And it is a fact, I think, that many people, by responding to this message, really have achieved a higher level, century after century, through all the years of Christian history. Human nature can be changed by faith, beginning with the faith that change is possible. But nothing is faith that does not issue in endeavor.

How much can human nature be changed? How much can it be changed today, to meet our present situation? The answer can be given in a single word: *enough!* Human nature can be changed enough to save us—if we are willing for it and determine that it shall.

19

The Power to Choose

WE ARE TOLD that there is much more fatalism than there used to be. There are more people, that is to say, who regard themselves as being in the grip of circumstances and who feel that they have no part in deciding their own destiny. Yet, they are helping to decide it every day. Even a fatalistic attitude is a contribution to decision— decision by default. For the truth is that the future is being shaped every minute, not only by statesmen and leaders but by what is happening in the minds of the people. Theirs is the decision—theirs above all—that will make or break the future of the world.

Nor are they choosing only when they concern themselves with what should be done about peace and war or the settlement of international issues. They are choosing in everything whatever which determines their own quality, their own character, their own convictions, their standards of behavior. Issues are decided not only by what we think, or how we vote, but by what we are. If we decide— fatalistically—that there is nothing we can do about ourselves, that we are powerless, that we are doomed to be what we always have been and that no effort will avail us in improving our own quality, deepening our courage, laying hold upon faith: then, by so believing we shall have *made* ourselves powerless, for such believing is itself a choice.

And these choices are being made every day. Ordinary people all over the earth are deciding the human future by what they accept or reject in the secrecy of their own hearts. They are deciding it not only by what they are willing to do to defend their civilization and its values, but by choosing the extent to which, *within themselves*, they incorporate these values.

The last thing in the world I would wish to do is to minimize the importance of what can happen when the great of the earth are assembled in the councils of nations; it is of crucial import. But not more so than the equally vital decisions which are being made by ordinary people day by day, and which these people hide in their hearts.

None of this is new, however, except in context; faith and fatalism have been in conflict since the dawn of history. It is true that the issues at stake are now of unparalleled magnitude; but the battle between these two alternatives is as old as the struggle within the heart of man.

Even in the relatively peaceful nineteenth century, people were preoccupied with the problem of inevitability; not only philosophers, who have always been concerned with it, but ordinary people such as those who gave so warm a welcome to Fitzgerald's famous translation of the *Rubaiyat* of Omar Khayyam. That was in 1859, the same year that Charles Darwin published *The Origin of Species.* There is no difficulty in understanding the popularity of the famous *Rubaiyat,* especially in the beautiful translation produced by Fitzgerald—a translation, it is said, that surpasses the original. But one can respond to its beauty without endorsing its philosophy. One can inquire why Omar believed as he did, and one can ask why others so believed.

Life's but a chequer-board of nights and days
Where Destiny with Men for Pieces plays:
Hither and thither moves and mates and slays,
And one by one back in the closet lays.

Who was the man who penned these lines? And what gave
him such opinions?

Omar Ibn Ibrahim al-Khayyam (to use only part of his
full name) was born some time in the eleventh century
at Nishapur. The name Khayyam means tent-maker, so
that he must have been a tent-maker's son. One of his
fellow students at a famous Persian school became Vizier
to the Shah and was able to get Omar a pension for life so
that he could pursue his study of astronomy. Eventually,
he became Astronomer-Royal and did important work
both in astronomy and mathematics. From time to time,
he wrote one of his quatrains, each one a distinct poem.
It is only in translation that all the verses are gathered
together to make a unity.

Now, it seems to me very interesting that Omar was an
astronomer, for if anything is calculated to make human
events seem trivial and at the same time predestinate, it
is the study of astronomy. The farther we look into the
infinite vastness of space, the more our earth becomes a
mere speck of dust. It was an astronomer who said that if
God may be presumed to exist, and if he sent an angel to
look for the earth, it would be like sending a child to pick
out one particular grain of sand on a ten-mile beach. It
was looking at the stars that made Thomas Hardy, author
of *Jude* and *Tess,* finally convinced that human affairs
were of no significance except to the particular generation
of humans who happened for the time being to be living
out their little lives.

When I think of this, I am reminded of a group of students from a girls' college who were taken to a famous observatory. The astronomer who was conducting them around happened to mention that certain stars might some day explode. "Oh dear," said one of the girls. "Do you think it might kill *me?*" "You little idiot," the astronomer replied, "what would it matter if it did?" Astronomers of the lesser echelons can sometimes get that way, it seems. Perhaps it is a good way to get. But for myself, I am not so sure. Had I been present at the observatory, I would have insisted upon explaining to the astronomer just why it might be important if the girl who asked the question were killed by an exploding star. Mere size or mass or distance is not the inevitable measure of importance. One living being, even a rather irritating sophomore with a giggling concern for her own ego, may be more important than all the exploding stars in the Universe. Is it an immensity of space that has significance or the mind that contemplates it? Is it the fire of distant suns or the flame of inner life?

At any rate, if Omar Khayyam had been a modern astronomer, he would have had to grant that even in the physical universe itself, there is what might be called an element of spontaneity. He might have been willing to listen to some of the modern philosophers, such as Alfred North Whitehead, assuring us that what takes place in the mystery of the mind can modify a whole physical organism, such as a human body, until the ultimate particles that make up its atoms and molecules are powerfully affected. Mind—a much greater mind than our own—could be doing that with the physical universe. I do not, however, go into that. The only point I wish to make is that the idea of a deterministic universe is out of date. It is not that the question has been settled but that it has been completely *unsettled*. So that whereas in the nineteenth century, science supported fatalism (or tended to do so), in the twentieth century science must leave it as a very open question.

It may be that before the twentieth century ends—if violent events do not too much disturb its continuity—popular understanding will catch up with the progress of science and it will be seen that the earlier supposed supremacy of the physical universe is giving way to the supremacy of mentality: that is to say, to life as it manifests itself in the mind of man.

After all, the Universe is, so far as we know it, nothing more than our total experience of what arranges itself in our minds. We do not find our experience in the Universe; we find the Universe within our experience. It is altogether beside the point to talk of God sending an angel to find a particular speck of dust called earth. It is not a speck of dust that we start with; nor is it the Universe itself. We start with life, and life is what we experience.

No one has ever seen the Universe. The only way of knowing anything about it is through the mind. And what the mind knows is only certain relationships of time, space and motion, which must be expressed as mathematical abstractions—abstractions which only the mind, and the rather exceptional mind at that, can understand. These abstractions neither prove fatalism nor disprove it. The attempt, therefore, to bolster up fatalism by the evidence of science is considerably out of date.

But at this point, there may be some modern Omar among my readers who will say: "Very well, let us leave science out of account. Let us forget the entire question of the ultimate nature of reality. What about experience?

What about life as we know it, life as history records it, life as we find it in experience? After all, even the original Omar knew something of life—much more, as a matter of fact, than he did about astronomy."

This challenge, I think, should be accepted. From time immemorial, men have believed in the gray Fates weaving the web of events. The Greeks put the famous three sisters, Clotho, Lachesis and Atropos above the gods themselves. These three sisters, daughters of Themis, who was the symbol of immutable natural law, spun the threads of destiny and, shears in hand, cut them through at pleasure. Greek drama is full of the interplay of fate. In the last analysis, all that happens is inevitable. Nothing could really have changed it. From the viewpoint of the casual observer, the characters in the play go about as though they were making free choices; but the playwright makes it clear that they are deceiving themselves. None of them is really free. Not even the gods can countermand the Fates.

In the modern world, we have another way of putting this. If we think of individuals, we say that they are predetermined by heredity and conditioned by environment. When we think of mankind as a whole, we speak of such things as the economic determination of history; or, if it is not economic, it is likely to be something else no less deterministic. Perhaps at the present moment we have in mind that mankind has never absorbed an important new invention—such as the atom bomb—without a maximum of havoc in the process. And so we expect that what has happened before will prove the index to what will happen again. There is little we can do about it, the fatalist will say. It is predetermined.

First, however, let us think about the individual. If heredity and environment completely determine what a human being must be, then truly we are helpless. For no one can choose his own grandparents. Nor has any way been found, nor ever will, of going around inspecting family trees until we find one that we like, and then adopting it. There is not a thing that we can do about our own heredity. We are in the position of Pooh-Bah in the Gilbert and Sullivan operetta, *The Mikado,* who, when he is asked how it is that he is always so disdainful, laconically replies, "I was born sneering." Everybody is born with tendencies—a complete set of them. There is hardly a doubt of it. And when it comes to environment, the situation is much the same. The psychologists tell us that the first few years of early childhood "condition" us more than all the years that follow. It may be so. And certainly we cannot choose the environment in which we grow up as little children.

But do these factors so control us that we have no freedom? There is considerable testimony to the contrary. Whatever may be the limitations, and whether theoretical or actual, men and women for thousands of years have believed that they were carrying their lives to fulfillments of their own choosing. Some have succumbed, of course, remaining prisoners of the situations in which they found themselves. Others have risen above their situation—fought their way out—and achieved a signal triumph. Helen Keller, for example, entirely defied the limitations imposed upon her by heredity; blind, deaf and mute, she nevertheless taught herself to "see," "hear" and "speak" with her hands, and with remarkable facility.

No matter what we say is our opinion, for all practical purposes we assume that we are free to choose—upon the basis of common sense. If I turn my car, in spite of sig-

nals, into a one-way street, and presently tell the policeman who arrests me that it was all because of an inherited
contrasuggestibility that I have been unable to overcome,
he will say, "Too bad," but go on writing the ticket. If I
appeal to the judge on the ground that I had an unhappy
childhood which made me resistant to authority, he may
send me to a hospital for observation. If, as a last desperate measure, I translate for him the French proverb that
"to understand all is to forgive all," he may cite me for
contempt of court and take away my license. The assump-
tion he will go upon is that I turned into a one-way street
when I might have kept out of it. And I think he could
be right.

I know as well as anyone that if we carry the question
into the forum of philosophy we can find it very controversial. I am aware, also, of the psychology of the subject.
Just the same, I insist that in the end, no matter what the
limitations, most of us presume that we have a sufficient
degree of freedom to affect considerably our own condition and decide in important measure the direction of our
future.

It is no different when we consider the future of the
world. Anyone can give reasons for thinking that no matter what we do, we may fail. But it is also a fact that if
we decide to win, we may succeed. The one thing that
makes failure most likely is the fatalism of people who say
it is inevitable—or who, shrinking from actually saying it,
nonetheless believe it. No one who knows anything about
history will deny that there are limitations on our choices.
But on the other hand, can we deny that choices can be
broadened if we decide upon it—or that in default, they
will be narrowed? This is what has happened in the past.

Is it not a fact of experience that one man has sometimes influenced the minds of millions by the words he has spoken at a critical juncture, and that one group of purposeful people, knowing their aims and being determined upon them, have mastered a trend of events? Anyone who wishes to disparage such a possibility must explain away what, as we have already seen, was done by the early Christians—or by Jesus himself. "Faith," said Jesus, "can remove mountains." He was entirely right. Mountains *can* be removed, even though it has to be a shovelful at a time. The decision is not in the blind, insensate, mindless substance of the mountain: the decision is in the minds of men.

I like the story that is told of Professor Toy of Harvard University, who was a pioneer in giving the world the modern understanding of the Bible. He was told that his task would be hopeless. Prejudice would build a wall against him that he could never remove. "Why," they said to him, "you cannot change people's views about the Bible! You couldn't do it in a lifetime; it would take five hundred years." But one day, Professor Toy faced his class and began his lecture with the following remark: "I have been told that it may take five hundred years to change the current view about the Bible; I am beginning this morning!"

It may take a tremendous effort to bring mankind through the present crisis; after that, it may take thousands of years to bring it up to the highest levels of idealism. "If so," says fatalism, "let's give up right away." "Nothing of the kind," says faith, "let's begin at once."

If anyone supposes that this is the view of a moralist and therefore biased, or that it would not be supported by a colder, more impartial mind, let me quote him one of the frostiest minds of this or any generation, Mr. Bertrand Russell. Assuredly, Mr. Russell is no optimist; he has been widely known as one of the world's most eloquent pessimists. Yet this is how he concludes an opinion on this particular subject: "The issue is the most momentous with which mankind has ever been faced. If it is not solved, war will exterminate the civilized portion of mankind . . . How it can be solved is clear; the difficulty is to persuade the human race to acquiesce in its own survival. I cannot believe that this task is impossible."

"*I cannot believe*," he says, "*that this task is impossible.*" He cannot accept a fatalistic doom. He has faith in the possibility, the attainability, of the world we want. What is necessary is that "the human race acquiesce in its own survival." For we, ourselves, shall decide it.

Even Omar Khayyam makes a suggestion that could point the way, little as he may have intended it. It is in the verse that goes:

Ah, Love! Could'st thou and I with Fate conspire
To grasp this sorry Scheme of Things entire
Would we not shatter it to bits—and then
Remould it nearer to the Heart's Desire!

Why not? Why not with Fate conspire? Why not grasp all the sorriness in creation and shatter it to bits? Why not remold it—the world and everything that's in it—nearer to the Heart's Desire? What has life been doing for millions of years but just that?—at first in what seems to be a blind, groping way; later with clearer aim and more fully conscious purpose? What is it that is making the struggle so inescapable in the world today if it be not that the world will not surrender hope, will not give up the heart's desire?

Why not believe, then? And believing, venture? The path to victory is a path that victors choose.

20

What Must We Do to Be Saved?

IN THE DAYS of our fathers, when the concern of religion was more with a future world than with the present one, it would have been assumed that anything said under the above heading would have had to do with other-worldly salvation. In short, the theme would have been the means by which hell could be escaped and heaven enjoyed.

Our own concern requires a different frame of reference. It has to do with this world, not the next. It recognizes hell, not as a place of torture projected into another life, but as a condition of the life we are now living. Nonetheless, we need something of our fathers' moral urgency. We, too, must "flee from the wrath to come!" Indeed, the peril has become more literal. And in our case, as in that of our fathers, there must be a cleansing of lives and an unfettering of bondage. It may once have seemed to us that our fathers exaggerated the power of evil and made an obsession of their guilt. But unless we are blind to the present condition of humanity, it cannot seem so to us today.

How sure are we that we are even worth the saving? We are living too far below our opportunities, too much beneath the claims upon us. In this respect, we are not as far removed as we might like to be from the situation depicted in the opening paragraph of John Bunyan's *Pilgrim's Progress:*

As I walked through the wilderness of this world,
I lighted on a certain place where was a Den, and I
laid me down in that place to sleep; and as I slept, I
dreamed a dream. I dreamed, and behold, I saw a
man clothed with rags, standing in a certain place,
with his face from his own house, a book in his hand,
and a great burden upon his back. I looked, and saw
him open the book, and read therein, and as he read,
he wept and trembled; and, not being able longer to
contain, he brake out with a lamentable cry, saying,
"What shall I do?"

In a different sense than Bunyan could have foreseen,
a whole civilization is now represented by that symbol.
With a great burden upon its back, it turns and reads in
the book of fate, and fearful and trembling, cries out,
"What shall I do?" Sometimes the question is a despair-
ing lament and nothing more, as though there were no
answer. Yet, there *is* an answer. If we really want the
answer and are willing to be such people as are worth
saving, we can be saved simply by using the means that
are at hand.

We are like some shipwrecked sailors I once heard of,
who rowed their lifeboat towards the mouth of a South
American river. With the passing of days, their fresh
water supply gave out. They knew that unless they were
soon rescued they would die of thirst. When their condition had become almost unbearable, they sighted a ship
sailing down towards them. They signalled and were
seen. But their thirst was so great that they could not
wait while the ship, with some difficulty, manoeuvered to
bring them alongside, and so, with what voice they had
left cried for water to be sent them. From the bridge of

the ship, an answering cry rang out, "Dip your buckets!"
They were utterly crushed by the mockery of such words.
Did the captain of the ship want them to drink the salt
water and increase their agony? But when they called out
again, the same response was given. And it was perfectly
sound advice. They did not know it but for over forty-
eight hours they had been rowing in fresh water. In the
wide estuary of the river, they had not been able to see
that they had left the open ocean far behind.

We are in much the same situation. The answer to our
need is ours for the taking. But if we are to see it, we
must have a state of mind in which seeing is possible. We
shall never see it if we remain imprisoned within ideas
that events have made irrelevant. Nor shall we see it if
we rebel against the truth of what is facing us.

When we are told, as we have indeed been told until
we are weary of hearing it, that we have entered a new
age, a so-called atomic age, requiring the application of a
wider range of aims and purposes, or that the world has
now become a neighborhood, and that this is so whether
it be a world divided or united, the thing that we need to
do *and have failed to do* is to see with perfect clearness
that this is not a form of words but a precise statement of
fact. It is not in the least a remote fact, like the informa-
tion that a new planet has been discovered or that some
one has set up a flag on the South Pole. It is a fact like
finding that we have moved from one climate into another
and must change our way of life accordingly. We shall
not be saved unless we become by actual, deliberate decision, the people of the new age, the citizens of the
changed world.

This means that many of the premises upon which
opinions and policies are still being based are not only

obsolete but definitely dangerous. They are just as dangerous as taking off from a high cliff with an intention to fly—but in a vehicle built to move only on land. Our circumstances have drastically changed and require of us a drastic adaptation.

Within this total adaptation there are lesser ones, but just as vital. If we live in the United States, for instance, we cannot be world-citizens as though we lived in Norway or Madagascar or Tibet. We are world-citizens who live in the United States. The consequences of that fact cannot be evaded. We have the power without which we would not have the opportunity. If we do not use the power, we shall lose the opportunity.

It is generally recognized that this fact requires of us considerable military preparation. In the absence of it, we would soon be forced to surrender. In this respect, we must do what is needful or lose the opportunity completely. Yet, armed might, no matter how we regulate it, will never of itself ensure our safety and survival. We shall have to learn a practical benevolence, a breadth of outlook that is only possible if we are truly world-citizens and our outlook is appropriate to the new age into which we have entered.

It is this, constructively, that can win security for the future. But nothing that we do reluctantly or niggardly or too-little-and-too-late will aid us in that victory. World-mindedness means, as I have said, a scope of obligation and responsibility that were very little understood until recently. It means it in everything—in economics, in domestic politics, in foreign policy, in race relationships—in everything we do or refrain from doing. We shall not be saved unless this is the foundation of our policy.

And while on the plane of government it may be new,

at the level of religion it is very old. It begins with the
first chapters of the Book of Genesis—"Am I my brother's
keeper?"—and goes on to Jesus of Nazareth telling us that
our neighbor is anyone who needs us, anywhere at any
time, everywhere at every time, and near and far,
throughout the world. *What has happened is that practical affairs can no longer be conducted at any lower
level than that of this morality, this loftiest expression of
religion.*

Nor will it do if this is turned into a mere pious formula, a generalized sentiment, as though big words could
be the answer to our problem. It must be, on its own
larger scale, the kind of actual and specific salvation that
the Old Testament prophets preached, in the context of
real events. They knew what we must learn: that God
intends to do his work through deeds performed by actual
men and nations. Only such deeds can build a world that
will survive; only such deeds will save us.

But as well as this attitude—world brotherhood trans-
lated into policies and programs—something must happen
to us in personal affairs. We are too undersized in rela-
tion to our problems, too morally dwarfed in purposes and
aims. Under the stress of difficult conditions, the worst
instead of the best is becoming dominant in all too many
lives. There is too much clutching, grasping greed; and
too much hate. Not alone between sections and social
groups and in politics, but even within families. For more
than twenty-five years now, it has been my obligation, as
it has also been my privilege, to look into the lives of
people in almost all conceivable circumstances, and I am
seldom surprised by what I see. It seems to me unlikely,
therefore, that I am mistaken in what I am about to say.

There is less love in the world than there used to be;

and there is too much hate. Too much little hate and too much big hate. Too much malice, both hot and cold. Too much scorn. Too much of everything that freezes sympathy and kindness. I repeat: there is not enough love. There is too much of people against people. Pitting their inward strength—the desperate strength of gaunt, disfigured, starveling souls—each against the other. What we see is petty loyalties instead of larger loyalties, loyalties with no depth in them. And so, divorce statistics rise, and alcoholism as a symptom of emotional tension and exhaustion, and "nervous breakdowns," so-called, and neuroses.

It is similar to the situation we have cited in these chapters as a parallel and example, that which obtained just before Christianity began to penetrate the declining Roman Empire. We need, now as then, a new liberation of the human spirit. We need love again: not the feeble pulsing of desire that modern songs are sung about, or the caricature that many people have accepted as the real thing. But love as the Apostle Paul wrote of it. The love without which no merit could avail and no virtue endure. The love "that never faileth."

Without a spiritual liberation to a higher level, we shall not be such people as deserve to be saved, and we shall know it. So that no matter how much we beat the air in pretence, we shall *let* ourselves be lost. We must have *within ourselves* faith in our own promise, confidence in our own worth; and they must be *real*.

For this, our need is urgent. If we are to be saved, it must begin in personal lives, transform homes and change communities, and thus flow out into the world. A time of cruelties and atrocities must become a time of restored humaneness. People must care as they have forgotten to

care. Gentleness must come back into life—even while the
realities are still harsh. These things must happen to us
or we shall not be human enough for the task before us.
We shall not be fit to be saved.

Do we see any hope of these things? Let me return to
those first paragraphs of *Pilgrim's Progress* from which I
quoted at the beginning. When the Pilgrim had made up
his mind to be saved, if it were possible, he met an
Evangelist who offered to show him the way. And pointing with his finger over a very wide field, the latter inquired, "Do you see yonder wicket-gate?" "No," said the
Pilgrim. Then said the other, "Do you see yon shining
light?" And after the Pilgrim had looked intensely and
for a long while, he said, "I think I do." Then said the
Evangelist: "Keep that light in your eye, and go up directly thereto; so shalt thou see the gate; at which, when
thou knockest, it shall be told thee what thou shalt do."

And there it is! For us as for the pilgrim of Bunyan's
parable. You start with what you see, even though it be
only a faint light; and "go directly thereto." Then, presently, you will see the gate, and the way will be plainer
to you when you have passed through.

To be saved, we *must* abandon in spiritual matters the
delusion that we can be picked up by some sort of
heavenly chariot and driven away from our woes. We
must always start exactly where we are, and proceed to
do the first things that raise our standards and improve
us in character. We must make for that 'shining light,'
even though it seem a faint one. It may mean expunging
a prejudice, expelling a bitterness, foregoing a mean intention, deciding upon a generosity—whatever is *real* can
really get us started.

We shall begin to be saved, our civilization and all its

people, when we *really* turn our backs upon what we must leave behind, and set our steps towards the future's guiding light. But it must be a real journey with all that goes with a real journey, including its burdens and sacrifices. It must be a journey to which we are altogether committed: a journey that removes us from the crumbling world that nothing can preserve and takes us onward to the world our firmness of resolve shall build.

21

The Faith We Never Lose

No MAN can live by doubt. He can only live by what he
does with doubt. When he acts—and living is impossible
without activity—he is bound to act upon some basis of
belief. He must at least believe that life and work are
worth continuing. As a matter of practical fact, however,
he will find himself believing a great deal more. He cannot live alone; he must live in a human society. And so he
must trust some other people—trust them when he buys
his food or has it cooked, or when he takes a journey, or
consults a physician—or relies—however small the measure—upon his friends.

As he cannot live without what other people do for
him, he must trust the reliability of the things they do.
He must believe that there is something that holds the
human world together, even though it frequently lets him
down. He must believe that his own mind is in the main
dependable, although it sometimes leads him to the
wrong conclusion. If he doubted it—doubted it substantially and practically—his entire life would come to a
standstill.

The truth is that faith is just as inevitable a part of
human life as breathing or digestion. We live by faith because there is nothing else we *could* live by. Even what
we know—or think we know—is in the end sustained by
faith: faith at least in our own perceptions and trust in
our own reasoning—both of which can be inadequate and

carry us astray. Yet we believe in them. We do because we must. We could not move a step or do a single thing without this sort of faith.

Is that what Benjamin Franklin had in mind when he said, "In the affairs of this world, men are saved, not by faith, but by the want of it?" It is difficult to know. Let us admit it: his saying may have been more superficial. It may have meant no more than that the prudent man will serve his welfare best by not being trustful any further than he need. Yet, I cannot help believing that Franklin had in mind a hint of something more.

The words were written for *Poor Richard's Almanack* in 1758. If they had been written a quarter of a century later, in what Tom Paine called "the times that try men's souls" we could rely upon a richer vein of meaning. For in that time of testing, it was necessary to find a faith upon which a new nation could be built. It had to be adventurous faith. It had to be a faith that man contained within himself the power, the hope, the desire, the capacity, to build a commonwealth unlike any that had ever been built before. And this faith came painfully and achingly out of the misery and distress of the time.

Here we come to faith on a much higher level than we were thinking of a moment ago. When everything is in doubt there is no alternative but to be bold—to venture, even desperately. It is an interesting fact that the fathers of our country were nearly all skeptics. They were that by intellectual habit, by training, and even perhaps by temperament. Paine and Franklin, Jefferson and Madison, Adams and Hamilton—all of them, not excluding Washington—were men to whom belief came hard. They varied greatly in their personal characteristics, but none of them was what is called a natural believer.

Yet a day came when they ventured in faith "their lives, their fortunes, and their sacred honor." More than that, after weeks and months of doubt and fear, they gave a charter of hope to a new nation. Not that they were confident of its acceptance. They thought the Constitution they had produced was more than likely to be repudiated; but, they said, they had to raise up a standard "to which the wise and the honest might repair." Out of their doubts they made a venture of faith that at times, even to themselves, seemed fantastic. From the want of faith, faith had come. Because of what they were *not* able to believe, they were forced to discover what they *did* believe; more than that, they forced to gamble—to stake everything upon the outcome.

Could they have done it if they had not found within themselves the thing that faith proceeds from? Something at last mysterious, beyond all powers of definition, that made them trust themselves and their fellows? Made them do so in spite of a clear-eyed recognition of the factors they were up against. Out of a time of "the want of faith," faith came. Men who were confident and self-assured could not have done it. Men to whom belief came easily would have relied upon the affirmations they had never really made their own—had never had to fight for— and would have failed completely. They would have been demolished by the first setbacks.

Let us understand this if we can, for we, too, are living in a time that "tries men's souls." Let us get a firm grip of the truth of the matter. What is it? It is this: that beliefs we have taken for granted, faith that we have not had to win, trust that has never been tested, are not enough. They will let us down. To wish for faith like this --the faith that is enough (for some) when skies are

sunny and the world goes well—is to invite our own undoing. Whatever takes fire too easily consumes itself too
rapidly. *That faith lasts longest which comes hardest.*

It is seldom the faith that men begin with that saves
them, but what they do when they find this faith dissolving. Untried beliefs, supported only by unthinking
assurance, are likely to lead to our downfall. They are too
lightly professed, too easily come by. "God's in his heaven,
all's right with the world," is a very comforting reflection
—until the world goes wrong. Then where are you? This is
not the faith that saves us. It is too superficial, too
thoughtless, too accidental. It is the mere rationalization
of a temporary feeling of well-being. A man for the moment happy believes that all the world has been con-
trived to lead to happiness. He sees his own reflection in
his outer circumstances, his own smiling face looking back
at him out of the sky. But what does he see when his
happiness has vanished? Where is his faith when the
storm comes?

But suppose instead of this, he merely feels the *want*
of faith? Suppose he is not sure that anything in human
life is altogether to be trusted? Then he may do some
genuine thinking. He will find that he must begin with
fortitude, not over-confidence, and in every variety of
experience that comes to him he will try to discover what
is real, what is true, what is dependable. His want of
faith will be a goad that drives him towards a way of life
that can be tested. But will he proceed without belief?
Without a single shred of trust of any kind? He cannot.

It is then that he finds his real belief; and this is the
belief that he can build upon. If we doubt that this is the
sound approach, let us inquire of the books of religion
We will find, there as everywhere, that there is no ad

vance when life goes easily. It is out of distress, out of
doubt, yes, even out of despair, that true religion comes.

The words that bring us most comfort from the Bible
are invariably those that were first spoken in times of
tribulation. It seems that underneath all doubt, all hopelessness, all despair, there remains a faith, and this faith
is indestructible. When everything above it is swept away,
it is revealed—the solid rock on which the life of man is
founded. Or better, the undying flame, the flame of life
itself which cannot be put out. If we can know this, we
can know something that is altogether dependable. And
that is a great deal in a time like this.

In this discussion we have pondered upon a saying of
Benjamin Franklin's. He is perhaps the least mystical of
American heroes. Let us move, now, to the opposite extreme and consider some words of an idealist. In 1835,
Ralph Waldo Emerson wrote a letter to Thomas Carlyle
which contained these words: "Faith and love are apt to
be spasmodic in the best minds. Men live on the brink of
mysteries and harmonies into which they never enter, and
with their hand on the door-latch they die outside."

Faith and love are apt to be spasmodic in the best
minds! To come and go, fitfully, capriciously, incon-
stantly. For there are mysteries, harmonies, that we can
never quite unlatch. Then this must mean that sometimes
we shall feel an emptiness where once we felt a surge of
faith. That from time to time, we shall be overwhelmed
by doubt. Is this to be counted strange?

Then let us point to something stranger. The psalmist
who cries out from emptiness of heart, from anguish of
despair, always somehow remains a psalmist. More than
that, he turns his very outcry into music, his agony into
a poem, his heartbreak into song. The terrible experience,

without veiling for a moment the nakedness of pain, becomes sublime. "Though I go through the valley of the shadow of death, I will fear no evil." . . . "Thy waves and thy billows are gone over me." . . . "O, my God, my soul is cast down within me." Where in such lines does the beauty come from? What magic thing has happened to an outcry that can make it lovely?

Just this: there is a light in the spirit of man that never quite goes out. We can lose most of the battles and yet not lose the war. We can go on when our minds tell us there is no use in going on—because something wiser than our knowledge, something ancient, yet forever new, something older than the world and yet younger than tomorrow, tells us that we *can* go on, and that we *must and will*. And we do.

"If you can still hold on," says Rudyard Kipling, "when there is nothing in you except the will which says to you, Hold on . . ." Yes—that! And you *do* hold on! Why? Because, though you know no words to tell it, and though you have but little understanding of it, there is a faith that won't give up, a light that doesn't go out, a flame that never gutters.

"Men live," says Emerson, "on the brink of mysteries and harmonies into which they never enter, and with their hand on the door-latch they die outside." Yes, outside . . . *but with their hand on the door-latch!* And that's what it is—a latch, not a bolt. The door isn't locked. It's just latched. Sometimes the latch lifts to our touch and the door begins to open. Then the storm comes and blows it shut. But we keep our hand still pressing on the latch. Why? Because there is a faith we never lose. Yes, and also because there is always something that faith can take hold of.

Perhaps there is more than that: something that takes hold of *us,* that always had hold of us, that never has and never will let us go. Perhaps that is why we can turn despair into psalms and anguish into music. Because there is something that sang the song of life at the very beginning—sang it into a world that was without form and void, when darkness was upon the face of the deep; and sings it still; and will forever. Not one of us can get quite out of earshot of its song. This is the ultimate, the innermost, the final, indestructible reality of life. Because of it, we call the mystery God, and in its presence, we ourselves are living souls.

Why then, should we not venture? Why should we not set forth upon a voyage full of purpose even when the storm is at its height? This is the time when we *must* be venturesome. There will be doubt. Unquestionably. There will be fear. There always is. But what of it? This is the time when faith can grow, because this is the time when we can find out all over again what it is that gives us faith. Why not trust the faith we cannot live without, and trust it to the uttermost?

Always it is in the desert that a highway is proclaimed; always it is the wilderness that is declared to blossom like the rose. This is the prophecy of those who went before us; this is the testimony of those whose light shone brightest on the ancient paths of pilgrimage. When unbelief is pressing hard upon us, faith is never far away.

One of the best remembered of the New Testament stories is that of the man who came to Jesus and Jesus asked him whether he could believe. "If thou canst believe," said Jesus, "all things are possible." We can almost see the man standing there, struggling within himself. Presently, says the gospel story, he burst into tears. "Master," he said, "I believe; help thou mine unbelief!"

How well that must have been understood by Jesus—whose spiritual pilgrimage began in a wilderness and was to end in a Gethsemane; who was himself to cry out one day, "My God, my God, why hast thou forsaken me!" And who yet somehow knew that he was not forsaken!

"I believe! help thou mine unbelief!"—such is the natural cry of the human heart. For it is a stout heart, yet full of fears. It overflows with joys unutterable, yet aches with the emptiness of hopeless desolation. In such a heart, faith and love are truly "apt to be spasmodic." For "we live on the brink of mysteries," of mysteries and harmonies; and are full of inextinguishable yearning.

> We are children of splendor and flame,
>   Of shuddering also, and tears;
> Magnificent out of the dust we came,
>   And abject from the spheres.

Splendor and shuddering! Dust and the light of distant stars! And we find our way and lose it. We see the truth and are blind. We love with a love like the love of God, yet what we love most we are quickest to betray. We press forever against the door, yet die with our hand on the latch.

And still we know that we can go forward in new and fateful ventures. We know it when we have found the faith that takes us through our darkest hours; when we have heard the desolate silence broken, and felt a stirring in the stillness of despair. No matter what the buffetings of circumstance thereafter, and no matter what the force of inner conflict, we have found the faith by which all un-

belief is ransomed, the faith by which great purposes, no
matter what the obstacles, are undertaken, the faith that
is the living substance of the soul itself, the faith we never
lose.